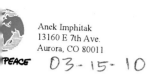

Anek Imphitak
13160 E 7th Ave.
Aurora, CO 80011

PEACE   03-15-10

D0031541

Women
and the Koran

Women
and the Koran

The Status of Women in Islam

Anwar Hekmat

 Prometheus Books

59 John Glenn Drive
Amherst, New York 14228-2197

Published 1997 by Prometheus Books

01 00 99 98 97   5 4 3 2 1

Library of Congress Cataloging-in-Publication Data

Hekmat, Anwar.
    Women and the Koran : the status of women in Islam / Anwar
Hekmat.
        p.   cm.
    Includes bibliographical references (p.   ) and index.
    ISBN 1–57392–162–9 (cloth : alk. paper)
    1. Women in the Koran. 2. Women in Islam. 3. Muslim women.
I. Title.
BP134.W6H45   1997
297'.082—dc21   97–21860
                                                                CIP

Printed in the United States of America on acid-free paper

To my wife, Mary Mandal

CONTENTS

INTRODUCTION

I stood at the gate of fire [Hell] and noticed that the
majority of those who entered it were women.

—Muhammad[1]

This study offers a critical perspective on the social
status of women as described in the Koran and as
defined by Islamic jurisprudence. This undistorted,
straightforward presentation of the facts will reveal that
millions of Muslim females, under rigid and inexorable
Islamic laws, have been deprived of their fundamental
inalienable rights and driven into seclusion for many
centuries. These humiliating laws have played an
important role in creating the socioeconomic ills that still
afflict the Muslim world today.

The majority of Muslim exegetes and jurisprudents,

9

especially among modern writers and commentators on
the Koran, have held that Islam actually elevated the
position of women. They insist that the rights of women
are well recognized and protected by Islam, more so
than in other faiths. They point out that Islam put an end
to such barbaric practices as infanticide of girls. They
also argue that by giving a married woman the permission to dispose of her own property as she pleases, Islam
has promoted her standing. Some modern interpreters
of the Koran go even so far as to insist that in Islamic
communities men and women are treated equally.

It is the purpose of this book to show that despite all
such self-deceiving, dogmatic, and not infrequently
biased rhetorical statements, the social standing of
woman was demoted by Islam. Even today she is still
humiliated, abased, mistreated, and ignored.

THE KORAN:
INERRANT WORD OF GOD?

The Koran, the main source of laws concerning women,
is believed by the Muslim faithful to have been revealed
and dictated word by word by Allah (the almighty God)
to His Prophet, Muhammad, during the last twenty-
three years of his life. Nonetheless, those who delve into
the subject more deeply and study the Koran impartially
will find it very difficult to accept claims for its divine
origin. There are many historical and grammatical errors
as well as quite a number of contradictory verses in the
Muslim scriptures. For instance, in chapter (called *sura*

in Arabic) nineteen, which is the story about Mary and her son, Jesus, we read:

> Then she [Mary] brought him to her own folk, carrying him. They said: O Mary! Thou hast come with an amazing thing. O sister of Aaron! Thy father was not a wicked man nor was thy mother a harlot. (Koran 19: 27, 28)

This is indeed a great error. Mary did not have a brother by the name of Aaron. In fact, she did not have any brother at all. It appears that in this case Muhammad confused Jewish and Christian traditions. He may have heard that the sister of Aaron and Moses was named Miriam (Arabic Maryam) and mistakenly thought that that Miriam was the same person as the mother of Jesus.[2]

A similar mistake occurs in chapter three of the Koran. Here the mother of Mary (i.e., Jesus' mother) is described as "the wife of Imran": "(Remember) when the wife of Imran said: My Lord! I have vowed unto thee that which is in my belly [Mary] as a consecrated (offering)." (Koran 3: 35) Every Christian knows that the mother of Mary (Anne) was not the wife of Imran. In these instances, Muhammad clearly made chronological errors.

It is practically impossible to ascribe such mistakes to an intelligent, lettered man, let alone an infallible deity. Some of the verses of the Koran are so repugnant to logic and reasoning that they could only be attributed to an uneducated, fanatic person who had been secluded in his own small world, void of common sense, and igno-

rant of the social conditions of his contemporary neighboring countries.

Nonetheless, Muhammad, the founder of the creed
called Islam, believed that he had found the solution for
all the social problems confronting human beings in the
Koran. According to Muhammad, the Koran is the most
complete scripture ever given to humanity by God, and
he himself is the seal of all the prophets. The revelation
of the Koran to Muhammad is considered to this day by
many orthodox Muslims to be perfect, and therefore
there is no need for further messengers from God. Muhammad contended that his laws are immortal and his
jurisprudence would last until the end of time, without
any need for changes. Since he believed that he was destined by Allah to unite all the people of the world under
one religion, i.e., Islam, he found it necessary, and often
obligatory, to impose his rules and regulations with
harshness and not infrequently with a drawn sword.

THE BEGINNINGS OF ISLAM
IN MECCA AND MEDINA

To understand Muhammad's claims for the Koran and
its pervasive influence on the development of Islamic
society as a whole, and on women's rights in particular,
it is necessary to know something about Muhammad's
life.

He was born and raised in the desert town of Mecca
in what is today Saudi Arabia. He was in his forties and
married to a well-to-do woman who ran a trading/car-

avan business when certain powerful religious experiences began to overwhelm him. He became convinced that God (Allah) was speaking to him through the angel Gabriel, instructing him to recite a series of divine pronouncements and commandments, which he felt compelled to promulgate to his kinfolk and the citizens of Mecca.

For thirteen years Muhammad preached his new faith to his home-town people, but except for a handful of his close relatives and associates, no one seemed to be interested. His rich and influential uncle, Abu Lahab,[3] bitterly opposed him and, more often than not, ridiculed him. His guardian uncle, Abu Talib, kept his own creed and remained pagan. Another uncle, 'Abbas, did not embrace Islam until after the fall of Mecca, which left him no alternative.

The people of his home town seemed to be happy with their own religion and thus felt no need for change. Happiness and contentment are the final goals of all faiths, and the preaching of Muhammad, in the early days of his call, apparently could not touch the souls of the people who thought they were contented with their own beliefs. The number of converts during thirteen years' preaching was not more than a couple dozen, mostly among his close relatives and friends.

Muhammad, however, was not a man to give up so easily. In 622 C.E. when the pressure of rejection from his clan was more than he could take, he decided to leave Mecca and start afresh in a new city. One evening, he asked his cousin, 'Ali, to go to his house, put on his clothing, and impersonate him, while he himself, in the company of a close friend, discreetly left town and fled to Medina, some two hundred miles northeast of Mecca.*

Thus, in conspiracy with his cousin, the Prophet of Allah was able to deceive his opponents. He was not ashamed of his act either, because according to his newly proposed faith, plotting is a divine order and Allah is the best of conspirators: "And they [disbelievers] plotted, and Allah plotted, and Allah is the best of the plotters." (Koran 3: 54)

As soon as Muhammad settled in his new headquarters, and his fear of his opponents temporarily subsided, he changed his attitude. Muhammad, the moderate preacher of Mecca, became the stern political leader; the law-abiding person in his home town became a law-breaker in Medina. The man who admonished against theft and larceny turned into an outlaw in his new settlement. He formed a group of zealot followers and led them on expeditions to raid the caravans of his own clan, the Quraysh.

He ambushed and robbed them of their property. He shed their blood in the sacred month and against all the prevailing rites of ancient Arabia. He broke his vows, and made his followers do so when he thought it would serve his purpose. He lied and deceived the others and claimed that it was right and just because Allah approved of it. He beheaded several hundred prisoners of war, against the widely accepted chivalry of the

---

*Islamic history is dated by Muslim historians from the year of Muhammad's emigration from Mecca to Medina, 622 C.E. This event in Arabic is called the *hijra* (emigration), "Hegira" written in English. The abbreviation A.H. (for the Latin *anno Hegirae*) is sometimes used before Muslim dates.

Arabs, and divided their belongings among his soldiers. He captured the women and children of the ambushed and defeated tribes and sold them on the slave market.

> To achieve worldly domination, he has recourse to assassinations, he perpetuates massacres, he makes a heathen superstition the keystone of his faith, and delivers to his followers, as a revelation from God, a mandate of universal war; with every advance in the worldly power he disencumbers himself of that humanity which was a part of his earlier faith.[4]

In short, during the last ten years of his life, from the day he arrived in Medina, his image was stained with blood, plundering, enslaving, slave trading, and burning the crops of those who did not want to surrender to his commands and accept his creed.

In the long history of pre-Islamic Arabia, the period that the Muslim historians call "the barbaric time" or "time of ignorance (jahiliyya)," no Arab had ever shed more blood of his own people than Muhammad himself. Under the poor excuse of promulgating Allah's commandments, he did more harm than good. For this reason he was dubbed by his own clan "The Divider" (mufarraq), the one who divided his own people and raised one against the other. Those who migrated to Medina with him had to fight with their own clans, the people of Mecca. The antagonists were none but their own relatives and close friends: "Muslim against non-Muslim in Holy war and fathers against sons in civil strife."[5]

Muhammad of Medina was the tyrant, a dictator, a self-made mayor of the town in which a minority of

Muslims dictated the fates of many nonbelievers. He was the bandit leader, the messenger of Allah, the law-giver, the law-breaker, the saint, and executioner, all at the same time.

> When he was at the head of the robber community [in Medina], it is probable, that the demoralizing influence began to be felt. It was then that men who had never broken an oath learned that they might evade their obligations, and that men to whom the blood of clansmen had been their own, began to shed it with impunity in the cause of "god," and that lying and treachery in the cause of Islam received divine approval, hesitation to perjure oneself in the cause being represented as a weakness. It was then, too, that Muslims became distinguished by the obscenity of their language. It was then, too, that coveting of goods and wives (possessed by unbelievers) was avowed without discouragement from the prophet.[6]

Muhammad died ten years after his arrival in Medina. The enmity and discord among his own people, which he helped to foster in his last years, seems to be reflected in the following lines:

> The wandering Arabs are more hard in disbelief and hypocrisy, and more likely to be ignorant of the limits which Allah hath revealed. (Koran 9: 97)

THE SPREAD OF ISLAM

Within a short period after the founder's death, Islam spread very swiftly in the Middle East and North Africa. But this is not necessarily evidence for the appeal of Islam; rather Muslim fanaticism paved the way for the desert Arabs. In hot pursuit of more goods and women, they raided the civilized world of Persia, Egypt, and Byzantium. They destroyed, plundered, raped, and massacred, enslaving women and children after killing the adult men. They conquered the affluent countries not because of the superiority of their creed over that of the conquered people, but because they were told the wealth of those nations was theirs. They believed that if they defeated their enemies, they were entitled to everything, including married women and virgin girls. And if they died in battle, they would enjoy the same blessing, even a better one, which was promised to them as a reward in "paradise."

No nation, community, or tribe embraced Islam on its own accord and without the fear of brutal reprisal. The new faith was forced upon them by the sword, and vanquished people had little choice but to accept Islam or suffer penalties. One penalty was a special tax (*jazya*), which non-Muslims wanting to retain and practice their own religion had to pay the Islamic government, under humiliating conditions.

The nonbeliever's life, property, women, and children were entirely at the mercy and disposal of the Muslim government. For example, they were not allowed to take as a wife a woman from their own clan if she had converted to Islam. Jews, Christians, and Zoroastrians were obliged to get off their horses if a Muslim passed by. Sometimes they were instructed to wear a special insignia as to be easily recognizable.

Islam means "submission" or "surrender"—submission to Allah and his messenger, Muhammad, by the pious Muslim. For conquered peoples it also meant submission to their Muslim overlords. But not all inhabitants of the expanding Islamic empire willingly submitted to domination by their Arab conquerors. The northern part of Persia, for example, resisted for many years.

PRE-ISLAMIC RELIGION AND ITS INFLUENCE ON MUHAMMAD

The nomadic desert dwellers had worshiped a multitude of male and female deities for many centuries before the Arab Prophet was born. Al-Lat was a goddess widely revered on the Arabian peninsula. Some scholars maintain that the word *al-Lat* is possibly derived from the Babylonian god Allata.[7]

Among the nomadic Arabs, the word *El* (or *Il*) was generally used to designate gods or deities. This is an old Semitic word which is found in different combinations such as *Beth-El* in Hebrew, which means the "house of God." Allah is a contracted form of *al-Ilah*. *Al* is a definite article used with all proper nouns, such as *al-Medina* (city) and *al-Islam* (Islam), and is preserved in English words such as Algeria, algebra, and so on. The definite article was also affixed before the names of deities. The ancient Arabs believed that Allah was a male god and therefore the father of three female deities, al-Lat, al-Uzza, and al-Manat. Hubel was also the city god of Mecca.

Thus, the word *Allah* was not coined by Muhammad. One can find many examples of this proper name in pre-Islamic literature. This word was used repeatedly among the pagan Arabs, especially with other combinations. The three daughters of Allah are even mentioned in the Koran: "Have you thought upon al-Lat and al-Uzza and al-Manat, the third, the other? Are yours the males and His the females?" (Koran 53: 19–21)

According to Muslim chronologists, Allah was the tribal god of the Quraysh, Muhammad's own clan.[8] But at certain religious ceremonies held in pre-Islamic days, many of the tribes would call themselves "the family of Allah."[9] In ancient Arabia, the deity of each tribe was respected according to the social status of that tribe. When the Quraysh clan became the overlords of Mecca, their god, Allah, was elevated to a supreme position and equal to the most important deities of Arabia, such as al-Uzza, al-Lat, and al-Manat.

We have clear proof that Allah was worshiped in Arabia before the time of Muhammad. Pre-Islamic personal names often contain the name of Allah as an element. It was the custom among the Arabs, in order to show their respect to their gods, to name their sons "the servant" or "the slave" of such and such deity. Muhammad's grandfather named his sons 'Abd-Allah and 'Abdul-Uzza, the slaves of Allah and Uzza, respectively, the father and daughter deities of his clan.

'Abd-Allah was Muhammad's father. He died before his son was born. Muhammad's own cousin, from his mother's side, was called 'Abd-Allah ben Djahsh (slave of Allah). His brother was 'Ubayd-Allah (humble servant of Allah). This brother migrated to Abyssinia as a Muslim, but there he became fascinated by Christianity, and subsequently repudiated Islam to become a Christian.

Another man whose name was associated with Allah before the time of Muhammad was 'Abd-Allah ben Djudan, a Qurayshite notable of the clan Tayn ben Murra; he lived at the end of the sixth century of our era.[10] He acquired a fortune through the slave trade. 'Umar, the close associate of the Prophet and the second caliph, had two sons, 'Abd-Allah and 'Ubayd-Allah, born before Islam.

Thus, Muhammad universalized Allah as the Supreme Being because this god was the tutelary deity of his own clan and his own father was named "the slave of Allah" ('Abd-Allah).

STONE WORSHIP, THE KA'ABA, AND PILGRIMAGE

The Ka'aba was the sanctuary in Mecca where the different pre-Islamic deities were worshiped. Among the images of the various gods and goddesses, the image of Allah was preserved alongside those of the female deities mentioned above. The sanctuary of Mecca, like any other house of god among the Semitic peoples (e.g., Beth-el), was in a rectangular shape and for this reason the Arabs called it Ka'aba, which is an Arabic word meaning "cube." Some scholars maintain that the word means house and they have suggested that it comes from an Ethiopic word meaning double or two-storied building.[11] But this does not seem to be correct, as the Arabic meaning of Ka'aba very clearly signifies rectangular.

The different idols were placed either around the rectangular structure in the open air or inside a niche (*qibla*) under the vault. It is believed by some circles that the rectangular structure was probably constructed after the shape of the typical nomad's tents. The Ka'aba dates back to the second century C.E.; thus, contrary to the text of the Koran and Muslim exegetes, it could not have been made by Abraham. The Old Testament makes no mention of the patriarch traveling to Arabia, much less building a sanctuary in Mecca! More importantly, there is no chronological or archeological evidence to prove that Mecca is older than the first century C.E., and Abraham, if he really existed, probably lived around 1800 B.C.E. The story was apparently fabricated by Muhammad himself to attract the attention of Jewish Arabs in the early days of his mission to win converts.

In the pre-Islamic period stones, especially soft and cube-shaped ones, were often considered sacred by desert Arabs and were venerated as the residences of gods. Nomads living in cube-shaped tents themselves probably thought the gods, too, would have similar abodes but of stone.

Among the many places of worship in Arabia, the Ka'aba was respected more than other sanctuaries because it held the Black Stone, which the pre-Islamic Arabs believed was given to them by the deities of the

skies to be worshiped. The Black Stone is thought to con-
sist of hardened lava, or basalt, but it is not easy to deter-
mine its real nature as it has been touched and kissed
rapturously by millions of people since it was placed in
the structure.[12] It may have a meteoric origin. Islam has
thus perpetuated the ancient pagan rite of stone worshiping by ordaining the pilgrimage to the Ka'aba as the
fifth pillar of the religion.

Millions of Muslim pilgrims visit Mecca each year to
pay tribute to the Black Stone placed at the east corner of
the structure. Mecca was already in existence in the
second century of our era, and it is recorded as "Mec-
oraba" by Ptolemy, the famous astronomer and geogra-
pher who flourished in Alexandria about 130 C.E.

From the early Muslim chronologists, we learn that
Qussay, one of Muhammad's early ancestors, developed a
carefully regulated cult for the worshiping of the sanctuary of Ka'aba.[13] He appointed two of his sons as the
supervisors (around 450 C.E.) of the cult. These two sons
were named, 'Abd al-Dar and 'Abd al-Manf, i.e., "the slave
of the house (of the pantheon of Ka'aba)" and "the slave
of Manf" (another stone idol), respectively. A number of
stone idols were placed in Ka'aba, each of which belonged
to a different tribe as their tribal god. The nomadic Arabs
would travel each year to Mecca to pay homage to their
clan's deity. The pilgrimage was traditionally made on the
last month of the Arabian calendar, the month of pilgrimage (*Dhu-Hajja*—the word *hajj* is perhaps the Arabic
equivalent to the Hebrew word *hug* meaning to draw
around).[14] The early nomads who visited the sanctuary
each year would go around the structure (the rite is called
tawaf) to pay tribute to the deities there.

In the months of pilgrimage and the month immediately before and after, the Arabs, according to an old custom, would stop all armed warfare with one another. No blood was to be spilled during those sacred months to make it safer for all the pilgrims to travel to Mecca for the ceremonies. In these sacred months, no armed robberies, ambushes, or vendettas were permitted.

The sanctuary of Mecca was known as the "harem," literally, the "reserved space"; for this reason the whole area of Mecca was also considered a sanctified territory. The word *harem* was used later for the women's quarters in large palaces, where usually more than one wife was kept. In this sense, it signified a private space to which no trespassing was permitted, allocated for women only.

In the month of festival (or *hajj*), each pilgrim brought his or her offering for a particular deity and sacrificed animals to please a particular god. Upon arrival, the devotees circumambulated the pantheon and then ran between two great stones called Safa and Marva upon two distant hills, which were believed to be the residences of a male and female deity.

Another practice in this festival was the ceremonial abstinences. The pilgrims would stay away from profanity, irreverence, and sexual intercourse, since each of these practices is prohibited in the presence of the gods of the pantheon.

The most diverse pagan tribes of the Arabian Peninsula would take part in the festivities of the pilgrimage. Since the performing of ceremonies was possible only when there was peace in the land, and as the Arabs were constantly fighting one another, the carrying of arms in Mecca during the pilgrimage was forbidden.

All of these ancient pagan rites survive in Islam today. Each year Muslims from all over the world make pilgrimages to Mecca during the Arabian month of *Dhu-Hajja,* and they perform the same rituals that prevailed several centuries before Islam.

The pilgrims put on a special white robe, circumambulate the rectangular structure in the middle of the Sacred Mosque, behead their animals while calling Allah's name, stay away from sexual intercourse during the ceremonial period, abstain from profane language, run between the two distant hills of Safa and Marva, and throw pebbles at the abode of Satan, a rock believed by the heathens to be the residence of the devil.

In fact, the pilgrimage ceremonies of Muslims today are in no way different from what Muhammad's ancestors and other desert Arabs did hundreds of years before him. Only the name is changed and the pagan cult has become Islamic rite. What Muhammad actually did was to perpetuate his ancestral customs and make them divine laws for his followers, calling it Islam.

There is only one difference: in pre-Islamic days, everyone was allowed to go to Mecca for pilgrimage—pagans, atheists, polytheists, as well as monotheists. Today, no one but Muslims are permitted in Mecca's sanctuary. And Muhammad's private god became the deity of all the clans.

Before Muhammad, each tribe had its own deity, but when they went to Mecca for pilgrimage, they would also worship, or at least respect, the other prominent gods. The followers of the goddess al-Lat would pay their tribute to Allah, her father. Those who believed in al-Uzza, would pay homage to her sister goddess, al-

Manat. Relations among gods were thought to be friendly[15] if the tribes were at peace with one another. When hostility prevailed, each tribe devoted its attention solely to its individual deity, ignoring the other members of the pantheon.

This is clearly seen from the life history of Muhammad's ancestors. As mentioned earlier, his great-grandfather, Qussay, named his sons after different gods. It is therefore obvious that at his time Arabian clans of the desert and especially clans of the towns were on friendly terms. When Muhammad started his preaching of Islam, his own clan, Quraysh, opposed him. His uncles, cousins, and all of his kinfolk were against him because he wanted to elevate his god, Allah, above all the other clan deities. When he saw the great opposition, he took a step backward and tried to quiet his adversaries by accepting their deities on an equal footing with his Allah.

That is why some of the early Muslim chronologists held that first Muhammad agreed to pay homage to the other deities, especially the three goddesses who were believed to be the daughters of Allah. But, later, after hostilities had broken out between him and many of the other Arab clans, including his own, he changed his mind and insisted upon the superiority of his god, Allah, the god of his father, 'Abd-Allah.

From then on he did not miss an opportunity to make Allah the supreme lord. He repeatedly affirmed that there were no other gods except Allah. One of the last chapters of the Koran, called "Unity" (at-tawhid), reads:

Say: He is Allah, the One! Allah, the eternal Besought
of all! He begotteth not nor was begotten. And there is
none comparable unto Him. (Koran 112: 1–4)

The point of this sura is to insist on the fact that his
Allah is the only god. Furthermore, he emphasizes that
Allah does not beget children, otherwise the followers of
the three goddesses, sometimes called the daughters of
Allah, would also claim the same privileges as the believers of Islam. Since there is no god comparable to him,
the other pagan gods or goddesses are not in equal
standing with Allah.

THE INFLUENCE OF
OTHER RELIGIONS ON THE
FORMATION OF ISLAM

The Muslim claim that before Muhammad the whole
Arabian Peninsula was polytheistic and that he, for the
first time, presented a new monotheistic religion in the
region is simply not true. Many centuries before Muhammad, the two great empires that exerted their never-
ending influence in Arabia—the Byzantine and Persian—were both monotheistic in their creed. Christianity
had penetrated into the north of Arabia, and Zoroastrianism as well as Manicheism had prevailed in the
eastern and southern parts of the peninsula long before
Christianity and Judaism came to Arabia. Moreover, various Jewish tribes were the residents of Medina and
Khaybar. By Muhammad's time, many of them had

business relationships with Syria to the north and Yemen to the south of Mecca. These people were later destroyed by Muhammad and their wives and children sold to the other Arab tribes.

A few Sabian inscriptions of the fourth and fifth centuries C.E. permit historians to conclude that Sabians believed in Allah as the supreme deity, calling him compassionate and the lord of heaven and earth, a title which is ubiquitously found in the Koran. "Above all," says Zwemer, "this tutelary and mediator god was the supreme deity whom they called Allah. This name occurs very frequently in pre-Islamic poetry on the inscriptions and in proverbs and personal names."[16]

For many years before Islam, the Arabs, though in a sense polytheists, were worshiping one supreme God, whom they thought was *ta'ala* (superior) to others. St. Clair-Tisdall says, "Although polytheism had even in a very early time found an entrance into Arabia, yet the belief in the one true God had never entirely faded away from the minds of the people."[17]

But perhaps the most important document proving the existence of monotheism among the pre-Islamic Arabs is the text of the Koran itself. The Koran talks about four groups of people (Koran 22: 17) who were monotheists and had their own scriptures, viz, Sabians, Christians, Magians (Zoroastrians), and Jews. Some of the Sabians' cult was incorporated into the Koran, such as thirty days of fasting, praying several times a day, and breaking the fast by observing the new moon (*fitr*). In fact, Islam and Sabianism are so interrelated that, "When Banu Jadhimah of Taif and Mecca announced to Khalid (Ben Walid) their conversion to Muhammadaism, they did so by crying out loud, 'We have become Sabian.' "18

Moreover, there are several hundred Persian words in the Koran which prove the influence of the Iranian cult in Islam. A great part of the Islamic belief regarding the resurrection and the hereafter is based on Zoroastrianism. The similarities between some of the Islamic rites and the Persian customs were so striking that some of Muhammad's opponents accused him of being taught by a Persian teacher. To this allegation Muhammad snapped back: "And we know well that they say, 'verily a human being teaches him.' The language of him at whom they aim is Persian, and this book [Koran] is clear Arabic speech." (Koran 16: 103)

As far as the story of the Jewish prophets is concerned, the Koran is a poor imitation of the Old Testament. Muhammad did not know any other language except Arabic. Some biographers held that he could not read or write even that language correctly and for this reason he was called *ummi*, which means unlettered. There are others who maintain that he was schooled enough to write in his native vocabulary. He was a merchant; therefore, he must have had some rudimentary capacity to read and write. One thing, however, is certain: he was unable to speak Greek or Hebrew, much less read it.

For this reason, he could not have read the stories of the ancient Jewish personalities in the Old Testament. He must have heard these tales from the people who were monotheists—not necessarily Jews or Christians alone—and adapted their ideas of monotheism. The difference in the accounts of the prophets in the Bible and the

Koran proves that Muhammad's source of information was not the Old Testament; rather he must have taken these accounts from the common people's hearsay.

Thus, monotheistic tenets were quite prevalent in Arabia at the time of Muhammad, and he did not present something unknown or extraordinary as a cult on the peninsula. "More fascinating and more tangible are the indications that in the last few pre-Islamic centuries, an Arabian monotheism developed."[19]

Besides these religious influences on Muhammad, he may also have come into conflict with the Hanifs, monotheistic Arabs who rejected all of the other Arabian deities associated with Allah. The Hanifs believed in one supreme God, but they also practiced an ancient cult. Among the features of this cult were regular pilgrimages to Mecca, sacrifice of animals to the Lord of the Ka'aba, and a belief in doomsday and the hereafter. It is possible that the presence of Christianity and Judaism provided the necessary requirements and conditions for the development of such a faith. The word *hanif* may be related to a Hebrew term meaning "to conceal, to pretend, to lie." Apparently, it is a Syriac word meaning "heathen" or "impiety."

It is not unreasonable to suppose that these people were probably acquainted with Jewish and Christian tenets, for the Hanifs claimed they were promoting the religion of Abraham. While believing in one God, they also maintained and preserved their old customs, which were mostly pagan rites. For this reason they were called Hanifs, or "heathens," because they could or would not renounce their ancestral beliefs.

The early history of Islam shows that there were at least four Hanifs among the relatives and close friends of

Muhammad. One who had a great influence upon Muhammad before he started his preaching of the new faith was Zayd ben 'Amir. It is narrated from Ibn Hisham (who reported from Ibn Ishaq) that Zayd's uncle persecuted him because he had denied his ancestral religion. He, therefore, left Mecca and traveled around the neighboring towns. He eventually came back and resided in the cave of Hara near Mecca.[20]

It is a well-known fact that Muhammad was a regular visitor to the cave, and sometimes he would stay there for days. There is no doubt that Zayd played an important role in shaping Muhammad's mind as he was developing his new faith. Muhammad always respected Zayd, and later even called him his precursor. The word *Islam* was used by Zayd for the first time, and there are many verses in the Koran that are merely a repetition of what Zayd had said earlier. For example this verse: "Lo! Religion with Allah is Islam [i.e., to surrender to Allah's will]." (Koran 3: 19)

Zayd died five years before Muhammad made his prophetic call. It is possible that Muhammad was waiting for his teacher to pass away before he began preaching these new ideas as his own. Apparently, Muhammad's association with the Hanifs, especially Zayd and Nufel ben Warqa (his wife's cousin), made the people of Mecca angry against him and they accused him of being a Hanif. It was against such allegations that Muhammad defended himself and the Hanifs. The Koran clearly explains Muhammad's tendencies toward Hanifs and his own beliefs when he states: "And (O Muhammad) set thy purpose resolutely for religion as a Hanif and be not polytheist." (Koran 10: 105)

Muhammad claimed that Abraham was a Hanif: "Lo! Abraham was . . . obedient to Allah, by nature a Hanif, and he was not a polytheist." (Koran 16: 120) According to the Koranic verse, the term "Hanif" is equated with monotheist, and so Abraham was also a monotheist. Moreover, Hanif is taken to mean one who is obedient to Allah, a submissive believer. There are many verses in the Koran in which Muhammad repudiates the idea that a Hanif is a pagan or a heathen. For example, he tells his adversaries that Abraham was a Hanif, therefore a Muslim. (Koran 2: 130–32) In another passage, he denies that Abraham was a Jew: "Abraham was not a Jew, not yet a Christian; but he was Hanifian and submissive, he was not of the idolators." (3: 67)[21]

In the light of the above, it is perfectly clear that Muhammad, through a close association with the Hanifs of Mecca, the most distinguished among whom were his relatives, became acquainted with their beliefs, which were called Islam. He became an ardent devotee of the new religion and, when fully convinced, started to act as a promulgator of Islam, which was originated by the Hanifs as a mixture of Judaism, Christianity, Zoroastrianism, Manicheism, and, last but not least, ancient Arab paganism.

It is interesting to note that not only his adversaries, but his ardent followers and even his close friends, pointed out to him on many occasions the inconsistencies in his scriptures. It was to impugn his opponents' accurate criticisms that he came up with a verse like, "This is a clear Arabic Koran with no crookedness in it." (Koran 39: 28; see also 18: 1; 41: 3) And again on another occasion, he tried to quiet his critics when he said: "But those in whose heart is doubt pursue, forsooth, that which is allegorical seeking (to cause) dissension by seeking to explain it. None knoweth its explanation save Allah." (Koran 3: 7)

■   ■   ■

Now that we are a little familiar with the origin of the name and cult of Allah, the sanctuary of Ka'aba, and the man who promoted the creed of Islam, we turn our attention to the status of Muslim women. We will try to find out what privileges, if any at all, Muhammad gave women in his new faith.

1

Muhammad and His Many Wives

Verily the chief among the Muslims [meaning Muhammad] was foremost of them in his passion for women.
—Ibn 'Abbas, the Prophet's cousin

The marital life of Muhammad and his behavior toward his wives, especially his inner desires for women in general, are treated in this chapter. We are given a glimpse into the private life of the founder of Islam both in the Koran and in its commentaries. The Muslim chronologists and exegetes who interpreted the Koranic verses in the first four centuries after Muhammad's death frequently provide us with valuable information regarding his treatment of women.

Regarding the total number of Muhammad's wives commentators differ in their estimates. The lowest figure

33

given is fourteen and the highest is twenty-one, but most of his biographers agree on fourteen. In any case, his harem accommodated more than a dozen wives concurrently, not including the young concubines.

As a polygamist in his late fifties, he enjoyed the companionship of teenaged girls, as well as mature women. According to the Koran, they were all given to him by the will of Allah. We know nothing of these women who shared the same man outside of their mutual life with Allah's Prophet. After his death, commentators do not mention any of them except for Aisha, his child-wife and his favorite, who survived in Islamic history to play a few minor roles.

The permission to marry so many women and live with them at the same time is granted to Muhammad by Allah in the following verses of the Koran:

> O Prophet! Lo! We have made lawful unto thee thy wives unto whom thou hast paid their wages [bride-price] and those whom thy right hand possesseth [slaves] of those whom Allah had given thee as spoils of war, and the daughters of thine uncles on the father's side and the daughters of thine aunts on the father's side, and the daughters of thine uncles on the mother's side and the daughters of thine aunts on the mother's side who emigrated with thee, and a believing woman if she give herself unto the Prophet and the Prophet desire to ask her in marriage—the privilege for thee only, not for the (rest of the) believers. We are aware of that which we enjoined upon them concerning their wives and those whom their right hands possess—that thou mayst be free from blame. (Koran 33: 50)

This passage makes it clear that Muhammad had special privileges; the choice was left entirely up to him to take as many wives as he pleased. By granting a special permission to his Prophet, Allah in effect abrogated his previous ordinance, which stipulates that a male believer is not allowed to marry more than four wives concurrently.

But rather than assuming that a divine revelation could be self-contradictory, it is much more obvious to conclude that Allah's words are simply Muhammad's thoughts in disguise. In other words, the lawgiver made two different sets of laws, one for himself, which gave him the particular privilege of marrying as many women as he pleased, and another set of laws for his followers.

Moreover, as it will be shown in the next chapter, no marriage contract is considered lawful in Islam, unless the amount of the bride-wage is clearly stipulated in it. But, again for Muhammad, this law, the Koranic Law, is not binding because he is allowed to take to his harem any woman who—in defiance of Allah's command—was willing to give herself free to him. This is indeed a special favor from his Allah, to break his own rule only to please his messenger. Four women gave themselves to Muhammad free of any price; he rejected one, but took the other three as wives.[1]

One usually associates this kind of double standard with despots, not with prophets of God. It is for this and many other similar reasons that most critics are doubtful about the authenticity of the Koran as divine scripture. The only difference between Muhammad, who claimed to be the helper of the poor and a human being like any other, and the Babylonian, Assyrian, and Egyptian tyrants of the ancient Near East is that they never denied their class privileges, so their rules and regulations were made accordingly. Muhammad, on the contrary, pretended to be a prophet, a messenger from God, a savior of human souls, the apostle of Allah who could guide his people to the right path of salvation. Nonetheless, the laws he decreed for himself were in every way more privileged than those governing the average man and woman.

The law which gave him absolute authority to marry any number of women his heart pleased was revealed in his new headquarters in Medina, almost four years before his death. By then he had more than half a dozen wives in his harem and was craving more. He had been about fifty-two years old when he arrived in Medina, and there he remained until his death ten years later.[2]

During this last ten years of his life, he acted not only as the messenger of Allah, but also as a political ruler, lawgiver, judge, and military commander. As an increasingly influential and powerful man, he married at least a dozen women and some biographers estimate above that figure. Most of his wives were young and in their late teens or early twenties, and one of them was a mere child of nine.

Of these women, one died before reaching his harem and three of them were divorced on the wedding night before being touched because they were too frightened. It is possible that he consummated marriage with fourteen wives and when he died, he had at least a dozen wives in his harem, not counting his concubines (slave girls).

Let us review what is known about each of these women based on the Koran and various traditional accounts (called *hadith* in Arabic) of the life of Muhammad.

KHADIJA

It is reported that he married his first wife when he was twenty-five in Mecca, where he was born. She was a widow by the name of Khadija and a wealthy, influential merchant, who employed Muhammad as a business agent. The goods of her business, mostly spices and silks, were imported from the east or from south Arabia and sent by a caravan to Syria and Palestine, which in those days were under the domination of the Byzantine Empire.

Muslim chronologists hold that Khadija was forty years old, but it does not seem probable as she apparently bore six children, which would be quite unusual for a woman over forty.

> Among the great fortunes of Mecca was that of a widow, Khadija of the Qurayshite tribe of Asad, who had been twice married to Makhumite bankers. With the help of her father, Khowailid, and of several trustworthy men, her commercial business, of which she was her own director, had become one of the most important firms in this Venice of the desert.[3]

Muslim biographers tell us that it was the wealthy woman who proposed marriage to Muhammad. Though this may very well be true, it cannot be ignored that the financial standing of the woman and her position in the affluent circles of the town might also have been a deciding factor in Muhammad's decision. Taking into consideration the fact the Muhammad was a shrewd businessman, as the course of events proved, and a man of high political ambition, we understand his acceptance of her proposal. He may have calculated that marriage to the wealthy widow, who was blessed with the fortunes of two previous husbands, could provide him with enough means to pursue his social goals. He was well aware that no political or social achievement is reached without enough financial backing. Later, when he lost his wife of substance, he tried to make up for the financial loss by raiding caravans and robbing other people of their property. As was mentioned above, his marriage to Khadija produced six children—two boys who died in their infancy, and four daughters, three of whom died before him and the youngest, who survived him by only six months.

The loss of so many children in their early years seems peculiar. As will be shown later, he managed to have another boy by one of his concubines, Mariya. But this boy, too, died in his childhood before the completion of his second year of age.

Why was none of his fourteen or so wives able to conceive by him? Except for Khadija, these wives were young and in their early twenties or late teens. Even his young teenaged wife, Aisha (the only virgin who married Muhammad), was unable to bring forth a child.

Was Muhammad afflicted by some sort of disease? Some of the non-Muslim biographers maintain that he suffered from leprosy, "which marked [him] by the deformities and by the disturbances of sensation."[4] Was

he affected by some venereal disease? Sexually trans-
mitted diseases were prevalent among the people in the
major towns of Arabia at the time.

But it is interesting to note that after the birth of one of
his male children, Muhammad was nicknamed Abu al-
Ghassem (the father of Ghassem). According to an old
custom, an Arab man distinguished himself as the father
of sons by taking the nickname Abu (father), followed by
the name of the son. As a cruel twist on this custom,
Muhammad's opponents had been calling him *Abtar*,
which is a humiliating word meaning "tailless," a man
without posterity. We have no way to prove or discredit
such an allegation. We believe that his nickname, Abu al-
Ghassem (the father of a son named Ghassem), was pur-
posefully given to him by his zealot devotees to stop the
disgrace and embarrassment caused by the insinuation of
his adversaries, who had nicknamed him "tailless." One
of the measures used to assess a man's capacity to be a
chief among the pre-Islamic bedouin Arabs was his
ability to father more male children than his close com-
petitors. It is not unreasonable to assume that Muhammad endeavored to demonstrate this capacity by marrying more wives, as will be discussed as we proceed.

As it was, his marriage to the wealthy widow was a
great relief to him. Most of the chronologists held that
his wife's fortune freed him from earning his subsistence:

> The marriage with Khadija gave Muhammad that
> ease of circumstances which he needed, freedom from
> the cares of daily life, the stay and comfort of deep
> mutual love, which for twenty years never failed him.

His wife retained the management of her wealth in her own capable hands, so that his mind was not burdened with the care of it. Whatever he needed was literally supplied.[5]

Thus, his wife's fortune was surely a favorable means in achieving his personal and political ambitions. As he did not have to work for his living any longer, he spent most of his time chatting with the people who had the opportunity to travel around and study the social lives and religious beliefs of other peoples outside of Mecca, even as far north as Syria, which by those day's standards was considered an advanced nation. As mentioned in the introduction, he developed a close association with Zayd ben 'Amir and his wife's intellectual cousin, Nufel ben Warqa. They held many enthusiastic conversations with Muhammad on the subject of beliefs and on the monotheistic religions of other peoples, such as Judaism, Christianity, Zoroastrianism, and Sabianism. Muhammad was thus able to pick up some information about the important events and tenets of other dominant religions in the area.

Khadija died after twenty-five years of mutual life with Muhammad. She was said to have been sixty-five years by then, although this is not certain.

Muslim apologists defend Muhammad on charges of polygamy and his great passion for women by pointing out that he was a faithful husband to Khadija. For twenty-five years and as long as she was alive, he did not care for another woman outside his marital life. The last thirteen years of his life, after his wife passed away, proved he was always attracted to women and had an extravagant passion for them. If he did not marry another woman while his first wife was alive, it must have been for reasons other than simply faithfulness, and devotion to his wife.

Unfortunately, the terms and conditions of his marriage contract with his first wife are not fully known to us. As far as we can judge, no biographer, Muslim or otherwise, has ever discussed the details of such a marital agreement between him and Khadija. But it is not unrealistic or illogical to assume that his apparent fidelity to his first wife could have been for the following reasons:

1. Khadija was a very capable, wealthy woman, and in view of the fact that she was from an influential clan of Mecca, it is highly probable that she had stipulated a certain clause in her marriage contract preventing her husband from marrying another woman. Before Islam women in Arabia were more independent than they are today under Islam, as will be shown later.

2. Financially, Muhammad was very dependent upon his rich wife, but it is clear that she would not have provided him with enough means to marry another woman. Even in our time and age, a young but poor husband is usually subordinate to his wealthy, older wife. In fact, except for a few years of his early life, Muhammad had no occupation at all.

3. Contrary to what Muslim historians may claim, polygamy was not prevalent during the pre-Islamic period in Mecca and most certainly not in Medina. It was Muhammad who universalized and institutionalized multiple wife-taking, mainly to justify his own practice when he fled his home town and after he

assumed power in Medina. The subject of polygamy in Islam will be treated more fully in succeeding chapters.

4. Muhammad may have repressed his sexual passions, not daring to bring them out in the open while his powerful wife was alive, but from the description he gives of paradise in the Koran, one can safely assume that the idea of enjoying the companionship of young, beautiful women was an innate quality and was always a part of him as long as he lived. As Johnstone says:

> Khadija was sixty-five years old at her death; it is not unfair to suggest that Muhammad was now yielding to passions which had hitherto been repressed and to which in his afterlife he gave free rein, with effects ruinous to the moral teaching of religion.[6]

SAUDA

Immediately after his first wife, Khadija, passed away, Muhammad married another widow named Sauda. She was the former wife of one of the believers who had migrated to Abyssinia (Ethiopia) with her husband on Muhammad's direct order. Her husband, after associating with Christians in that country, and comparing his creed with that of Christianity, abandoned Islam and became a Christian. After his conversion, Sauda left him in Abyssinia and returned to Mecca.

In accordance with Islamic jurisprudence, any Muslim man who changes his religion and thus becomes an apostate is considered divorced from his wife, and she is no longer considered legally bound to him. On her return to Mecca Muhammad took her as his wife and consummated the marriage. This took place just a few days after the death of Khadija, to whom he had, according to the Muslim apologists, always been faithful.

AISHA

But Sauda was in his harem no more than a few months when he married the little daughter of his close friend Abu Bakr, a rich merchant of Mecca who embraced Islam in the early days of the call. The girl, named Aisha, was only six years old when the marriage contract was made. Three years later, when Muhammad fled his home town and entered Medina, the little girl of nine was delivered to his harem. The apostle of Allah, in his passion to possess her, was in such a hurry that he did not even wait for nightfall; he asked the bride's mother to send her to his bedchamber in the morning hours after the wedding ceremony.

The child-bride, who very soon became Muhammad's favorite wife, had this to say about her marriage.

The Messenger of God married me when I was six years old and the wedding was celebrated when I was nine. We came to Medina and then I had the fever for a month. Then my hair, which had fallen out because of my illness, began to grow thickly again. Umm Ruman [her mother] came to find me while I was playing with my friends on a swing. She called me and I went to her, not knowing what she wanted of me. She took me by the hand and stopped me on the threshold. I cried out, "Oh! Oh!" until I was out of breath. She took me into a house in which were some women of Medina, who said, "Happiness and blessings! Good fortune!" My mother gave me into their keeping and they washed my head and made me beautiful. I was not frightened, except in the morning, when the messenger of God came and they gave me to him.[7]

According to this tradition, which is narrated by the wife and companion of Muhammad and believed by all Muslim exegetes and jurisprudents to be authentic, this girl was merely nine when she was sent to Muhammad's bedchamber, and she was horrified when she found out what was going to happen. One can imagine the physical pain and psychological agonies of a nine-year-old girl when this man in his fifties made sexual advances and deflowered her passionately.

Al-Bukhari, the famous compiler of the *hadiths* (traditional accounts of Muhammad's acts and words, supposedly going back to eyewitnesses), affirms the above story:

Aisha narrated that the Prophet married her when she was six years old and he consummated his marriage when she was nine years old, and then she remained with him for nine years.[8]

From the girl's own account and the reports of a number of Muslim commentators, it can be inferred that:

1. Child-marriage is lawful in Islam and the necessary contract can be drawn up between the guardian and the would-be husband even when the girl is no

more than five or six years old. In this sense marriage is nothing but the sale of a minor girl. We shall refer to this in more detail in the following chapter.

2. The consent of the girl is not a prerequisite for the marriage of a female child to a grown man over fifty.

3. Sexual intercourse of a fifty-year-old man with a mere girl is not something to be ashamed of. On the contrary, the act of Muhammad in taking a child as his wife set a precedent, which then became a tradition (*sunna*) in the Muslim lawbooks and jurisprudence.

4. Despite the fact that the girl was frightened when Muhammad approached her sexually, the Prophet went on to consummate the marriage regardless of the consequences. Whereas sexual intercourse with a girl in her childhood is a punishable offense in most countries of the world today, this deplorable custom still goes on in some Muslim nations. The girl was so small that according to the reliable Islamic biographers, she took along her toys and playthings to the Prophet's bedchamber. "The little girl was allowed to keep her toys and her dolls and sometimes the Prophet would play games with her."[9]

The age difference between Muhammad and Aisha was so great that the girl's father was younger than the bridegroom. In fact, Muhammad was old enough to be her grandfather. Apparently he was so taken with his new young wife that he bestowed a special nickname on her father, Abu Bakr, which means "the father of the virgin" or "the father of the camel's foal."[10] (Muhammad's adversaries mockingly twisted the surname to Abu Fasil, i.e., "father of the weaned young of a camel.") The result of Muhammad's lasting affection for the girl was that her father became the heir apparent to Muhammad's legacy. He succeeded his son-in-law after the latter's death as the first caliph of Islam. The word caliph —khalifa in Arabic—means substitute or successor.

THE FRUITS OF PLUNDER: WEALTH AND WOMEN

By now, though Muhammad had two women in his harem, he was not yet content. From his new base in Medina he began a series of forays in which he ambushed passing caravans. In one successful raid he gained possession of stolen commodities valued at more than one hundred thousand dirhams (the unit of money in Arabia in those days). He took one-fifth of the booty for himself, according to Allah's ordinance in the Koran, and divided the rest among his followers: ". . . whatever ye take as spoils of war, lo! a fifth thereof is for Allah, and for the messenger. . . ." (Koran 8: 41)

As chief of this marauding band Muhammad suddenly found himself financially in a better position. From the wealth of the plunder, he was able to acquire another wife. 'Umar, his close friend and companion, had a proud widowed daughter, Hafsa, a charming but temperamental eighteen-year-old woman. 'Umar was delighted to hear that Allah's apostle was interested in her; therefore, the marriage contract was drawn up between the father and the bridegroom, who once again was some years older than his father-in-law. The wedding was not elaborate, but he spent three nights on a honeymoon with his new wife.

In the fourth year after his emigration to Medina, Muhammad found a poor excuse to raid a Jewish tribe in the same town, known as the Banu Nadir. He besieged their quarters and let no water or food reach them. Then he set their crops on fire and ordered their fruit trees to be cut down, which was against all the prevailing customs of the Arabs at that time. When his followers objected and reminded him that felling trees and burning crops in that part of the world, where only a few inches of rain fall each year, is an unforgivable crime, he immediately invented the following passage: "Whatsoever palm trees ye cut down or left standing on their roots, it was by Allah's leave, in order that He might confound the evil-doers [the Jews]." (Koran 59: 5)

The Jews of the besieged tribe sent someone to negotiate peace, but Muhammad would not accept unless they left all their property behind and moved out. Each family or household was permitted to take along only a camel-load of their necessities excluding silver or gold wares. After they were forcibly banished from Medina, the Muslims, on direct order of Muhammad, took over the homes, farms, orchards, and gardens of the ill-fated people, plus their goats, sheep, camels, mules, and whatever was left in their homes.

This may be the first time in history that a man claiming to be a prophet, saint, and teacher of ethics was also a lawless marauder.

As a result of such a quick and easy victory, Muhammad was no longer willing to divide the rich booty among his followers; he therefore revealed the following verse: "That which Allah gave as spoil unto His messenger from the people of the townships, it is for Allah and his messenger and for the next of kin." (Koran 59: 7) By this simple device of revelation he was able to deny all of his followers the benefit of the foray and keep as much booty for himself and his relatives as he wished.

The rich fortune of the Jewish people of Banu Nadir provided Muhammad with enough means to contemplate expanding his harem once more. In less than six months after this episode, he married two women from his clan, the Quraysh tribe of Mecca, both of them younger than thirty years old. His harem now included five young women.

In the fifth year after the Hegira, Muhammad decided to destroy the remaining Jewish population of the town (known as the Banu Qurayza) and take over their property. He therefore surrounded their quarters and began a siege that continued for some time until the elderly people of the tribe finally decided to surrender in order to save their lives from his dreadful vengeance. Muhammad, however, did not want them to go unpunished. He therefore demanded that they be judged by an arbitrator, a man whom he knew, deep in his heart, was not very amiable to the Jews. The man who was nominated by Muhammad to act as an arbitrator was Sa'd ibn Mu'az, who happened to be suffering from a wound inflicted by the enemy's arrow in a previous battle and was really on the verge of dying. Aware of the enmity between the man and the ill-fated tribe of the Banu Qurayza, Muhammad could easily guess what the sentence of the dying man would be, especially since Sa'd ibn Mu'az was led to believe by some Muslims that his fatal wound was the result of the Jews, who had been secretly in touch with the enemy.

Muhammad ordered the dying man to be carried over in a stretcher from his house to a meeting in which the representatives of the besieged tribe were present. The arbitrator, Sa'd, gave his verdict as follows:

1. All the adult males of the defeated Jewish tribe must be slain.
2. Their women and children must be sold as slaves to the highest bidder.
3. All their property (camels, goats, horses, farms, orchards, household furniture, etc.) must be divided among the Muslims.

After Muhammad heard this barbaric verdict, he cried out in jubilant words: "You have judged according to the very sentence of Allah above the seven skies."[11]

According to the above statement, which has been affirmed by the early biographers and chronologists, Muhammad's Allah is seemingly as cruel and ferocious as his Prophet. "The women and children, torn from their protectors, were placed under the charge of renegade Jews."[12]

The arbitrator did not live long enough to see the outcome of his judgment; he died that very day. Muhammad ordered his men to dig deep trenches in the marketplace of the town, to be used as "common graves"[13] for the slain Jews. The captured Jews, with their hands tied behind their backs, were led to the edge of the trench in groups of ten. They were forced to kneel down and, with unprecedented savagery, were beheaded one by one while their kinfolk watched in horror and wailed in agony.[14]

The dreadful show continued the whole day in the presence of Allah's apostle, who seemed to be delighted. His close male relatives, 'Ali, Zubayr, and others, acted as executioners in this barbaric pageantry. The butchery started in the morning and continued until the evening under torchlight.

The number of murdered men, according to various accounts, was between six hundred fifty and nine hundred; most Islamic sources agree on seven hundred and fifty.[15] Among the captured was a young smiling woman who had thrown a stone from the roof of her home onto the Muslim soldiers. Muhammad ordered his followers to bring the woman to the trench and decapitate her, which they did. The chivalry of the pre-Islamic Arabs was lost forever after the advent of Islam.

After the trenches were filled with the heads and bodies of the victims, he instructed his men to fill them. The ditches were quickly smoothed over the remains and the carnage was thus trampled underfoot by the steps of the devotees. The captive women and children were paraded before Allah's apostle, who with the vainglory of a victorious bedouin chieftain, reviewed them with contempt. To him they were merely the booty of war.

There was a charming young girl among them by the name of Rayhana, who had lost her husband and all of her male relatives in the massacre. As soon as Muhammad's eyes caught sight of the wretched Jewess in the long line of women and children, an irresistible passion to possess her came over him. He signaled his soldiers to bring her as his share of the booty. "As they passed before the conqueror, his eyes marked the lovely Raihana, and he destined her for himself."[16]

The girl is reported to have been around nineteen and as she refused to embrace Islam, she was sent to his harem as a concubine: the honeymoon started the very night of the massacre and lasted three days.[17]

The women and children were distributed among the male believers and some were sold in the slave market. The property of the ill-fated people consisted of camels, goats, sheep, armor, clothes, and household furniture.

The massacre of the Banu Qurayza tribe proved that Allah's apostle was a bandit, a vengeful political leader, a merciless executioner, and a slave merchant. It also cast a long shadow over Islam. If this new religion was dedicated to advancing the cause of one god, as its founder claimed, against the idolatry and polytheism of the desert Arabs, why did Muhammad so relentlessly persecute first Judaism and later on Christianity and Zoroastrianism, all of which were monotheistic religions? With his increase in power, the real character of Allah's messenger began to manifest itself. One suspects that his underlying motive was power, not religion. As the leader of a gang of robbers, he sent his followers on numerous expeditions to raid caravans, ambush the different tribes of the desert, slay innocent people, seize their property, and enslave their women and children. The booty in these forays was enough motive for the greedy desert Arabs to join him.

In order to become a shareholder in the spoils bestowed by Allah, one needed only to affirm that Allah is the only deity and Muhammad is his messenger. By this simple formula the robber chief of Medina was able to gather more men around him and keep his little force in high spirits by giving them more share of the booty. He promised them both paradise after death and wealth and women in this world. With these incentives the desert Arabs who followed him had nothing to lose.

Gradually, as he got more powerful in his new head-quarters of Medina, the peace-loving preacher of Mecca disappeared and in his stead the party leader and author-itarian ruler of Medina came to light. His former themes of mercy and compassion are replaced with the unyield-ing decrees of the tyrant. Among the deeds of the great founders of religions, such as Zoroaster, Confucius, Buddha, Moses, and Christ, one can find nothing compa-rable with Muhammad's plundering of caravans, am-bushing of tribes, massacring of prisoners of wars, and enslaving of the women and children. Nor did any of these religious leaders have as many wives as Muham-mad. In these and similar performances, Muhammad is unique and unparalleled. No man of God was changed so much in so few years and in such a barbaric way.

In Medina, Muhammad's revelations are not as poetic and as heartfelt as the ones he recited in Mecca in the early days of his call. The Mecca suras of the Koran are quite different from the Medina suras, many of which are harsh, authoritarian, and tyrannical. A few examples will suffice.

When he robbed a caravan, he needed a law to divide the booty among his followers; so conveniently Allah fulfilled his wishes and sent an ordinance (Koran 8: 1, 41). When he raided the farmers, burning their crops and cutting down their date-palms, which was a for-bidden act in Arabia, he revealed a passage to sanction his unlawful act and mitigate the objections of his fol-lowers (Koran 59: 5). When he spilled the blood of innocent people in sacred months, which was against the long-preserved Arab custom, another revelation was brought forth to justify his folly (Koran 2: 217).

In the first two centuries after the rise of Islam, hundreds of thousands of men, women, and children in Egypt, Palestine, and Persia were taken as prisoners of war and sold as slaves. "When the sacred months have passed, slay the idolaters wherever ye find them, and take them captive, and besiege them, and prepare for them each ambush." (Koran 9: 5)

CONQUEST OVER THE BANU MUSTALIQ: JUWAYRIYYA AS BOOTY

Six years after the Hegira (December 627 and January 628), Muhammad set out to raid the Banu Mustaliq tribe.[18] They were rich and probably were contemplating a raid on Medina, though there is no proof of this except the accounts of Muslim chronologists. The tribe was ambushed near Muraysi, which was a well (or spring) near the coast.[19] The booty, according to Muslim sources, included: "Two thousand camels, five thousand heads of sheep and goats, and two hundred women."[20]

Muhammad's share of this booty, among other things, was a new wife. He chose the wife of the chief of the tribe, Juwayriyya, who by all accounts was a beautiful woman. She had lost her husband and all of his male relatives in the raid, and she was attempting to buy her freedom by paying a ransom.

The captives of Beni-Mustalik having been carried to
Medina, with the rest of the booty, men from their
tribe soon arrived to make term for their release. One
of them was Juwairya, a damsel of birth and beauty,
almost twenty years of age, and married to the chief of
the tribe.[21]

The girl wanted to pay the ransom and release herself from bondage, but she could not come to terms with
her captor, a man named Thabit. However, she was bold
enough to bring the case to Muhammad's attention,
imploring him to mediate between her and the soldier in
the dispute over the ransom money. As soon as the messenger of Allah met the pretty young captive, he felt passion for her and proposed to pay the ransom himself so
that he could take her to his harem.

Some, if not all, Islamic historians interpret this ges-
ture of Muhammad as a sign of his human character. But
this does not seem to be the case, because if he had
meant well, he could have paid the ransom and sent her
away to her father to continue her life as she pleased; or
he could have instructed one of his young bachelor soldiers to marry her—every one of them would surely
have responded favorably; or he could have ordered her
captor to set her free and get another share from the
booty in her stead. He did not do anything of the sort; on
the contrary, he bought her for himself. His motive in
this particular case was obviously self-serving. Her
youth and beauty had inflamed his passions. The record
of Aisha's reaction to this new woman confirms this
impression. According to the Muslim chronicler Ibn
Sa'ad, Aisha described Juwayriyya as "so cute that who-

ever caught a glimpse of her fell for her."[22] She appears to have been jealous: "By Allah, I had scarcely seen her [the captive girl] in the doorway of my room before I detested her. I knew he would see her as I saw her."[23]

Surely Aisha, as Muhammad's spouse and close companion, could judge her husband's behavior much better than later orthodox Muslim writers who tried to find a godly reason for the merely natural instincts of a man.

Would Allah's messenger have married her if she was not young and pretty? It is doubtful. Another story about Muhammad concerns his initial interest in a woman whose hair was reputedly long enough to cover all her body. Muhammad approached the woman's son and asked him if he could marry his mother. The mother and the son both agreed. In the meantime, Muhammad sent some of his close friends to investigate, but when he learned that she was "aging" he lost interest and cancelled the wedding.[24]

Thus the main reason for paying the ransom money for the captive girl was her lovely face and youth.

ZAYNAB

Perhaps the most scandalous passion that Muhammad developed in his late fifties was the sudden desire to take his adopted son's wife. This affair defied all the common laws and customs of the Arab community of that time.

The story runs as follows.

Muhammad's first wife, Khadija, had presented him with a male slave named Zayd as a wedding gift. Since Muhammad did not have a male issue, he freed him first and then adopted him as his son. This Zayd later married a pretty young woman from Muhammad's kin, who was called Zaynab.

One day Muhammad went to his adopted son's house unexpectedly. Zayd was not at home, but his wife welcomed her father-in-law in even though she was not fully dressed. Being his daughter-in-law, she probably did not bother to put on proper attire or to cover herself completely. Muhammad did not fail to notice the hidden beauties of his daughter-in-law, and after murmuring a few incoherent words, he exclaimed: "Praise to Allah, the most high! Praise to Allah, who changes men's hearts."[25]

It is obvious from the accounts of this incident that the girl's beauty aroused his passion. Muslim historians tell us that after seeing Zaynab's half-naked body, Muhammad left the house immediately in a state of confusion. Some chronologists report that Zaynab must certainly have overheard Muhammad's praise of her beauty, and she was proud of her effect on him. She even let her husband know how his father fell for her charms. From that day on Muhammad must have contemplated adding her to his harem.

There were, however, two main obstacles in his way: first, she was already married and second, she was the wife of his son. Koranic law (Koran 4: 23) is explicitly against the marriage of the father with his daughter-in-law. Moreover, the Arabs, through long-established custom, detested the idea of such a relationship, which they regarded as "dreadfully incestuous."[26]

But when you have Allah on your side, all such problems are easily solved. When Zayd heard the story of his father's visit to his wife, he went to him and proposed to divorce her. But Muhammad, who was aware of what his followers' reactions would be, apparently preferred to take an indifferent attitude, and therefore advised his son to keep his wife for himself.

Nevertheless, Zayd divorced his wife, perhaps because he feared the outcome of his opposition to his father, particularly when it meant another woman. Being a submissive believer and sheepish son, Zayd could not have opposed his father's will, even after being told to keep his wife. Thus, the first obstacle was removed from Muhammad's desire to take Zaynab as his wife.

In the meantime, Muhammad was looking for an opportunity to enable him to prepare the minds of his companions to accept the unprecedented action of his marriage to his former daughter-in-law. In fact, his passion for Zaynab was so intense that he could no longer keep it secret. This is manifested in the Koran. Graciously Allah revealed to him a divine pronouncement that gave him the permission to marry Zaynab. One morning he recited this new revelation before Aisha:

> And when you said to him [Zayd] . . . "keep thy wife to thyself and fear Allah," you concealed in your soul what Allah was about to display, and you feared man, though Allah is more deserving that you fear Him; and when Zayd divorced her, We did wed you to her, so that there should be no hindrance to the believers regarding the wives of their adopted sons. . . . The commandment of Allah must be fulfilled. (Koran 33: 37)

The above passage makes it clear that when Muhammad told his son not to divorce his wife, he really didn't mean it, and down deep in his heart he wanted him to repudiate his wife so that he might be able to marry her. It also affirms that Muhammad was apprehensive that his marriage to his former daughter-in-law would cause unfavorable repercussions among the believers: "and you feared man, though Allah is more deserving that you fear Him." In other words, if it was not for the sharp criticism and objections from some of the faithful, he would have proposed marriage to his former daughter-in-law immediately.

Did Muhammad play any role in his son's decision for divorce? Most probably he did, because if he had admonished his son not to repudiate his wife, Zayd could not have refused; he was his father, his emancipator, and the Prophet, and no Muslim believer defies the direct command of the messenger of Allah, let alone his devoted son, who believed in him more than anybody else. Zayd was the first man to embrace Islam. In fact, in the beginning of Muhammad's call, two people responded favorably to him—his wife, Khadija, and his adopted son, Zayd. ('Ali, his cousin, who was only a boy, and his long-time friend, Abu Bakr, also embraced Islam early on, but after the previously mentioned two.) Ever since Zayd accepted Islam, he was a devotee to the messenger and the creed. Thus he could not have divorced his wife without the approval of his father.

It is also unlikely that Zayd was dissatisfied with his wife, such that he would have desired a divorce from her, for two simple reasons: first, she was young, charming, and from a noble house, and second, the idea of separation started from the day that his father visited his wife in his absence. On top of that, Zaynab was a cousin of Muhammad himself, and it was he who had proposed to his son to marry her. Zayd must have loved her dearly.

Despite the revelation from Allah granting Muhammad permission to marry Zaynab, the scandalous act had its detrimental effects and wagging tongues could not be completely stopped from gossiping over the incident. In order to keep the image of the messenger of Allah as innocent as possible, later Muslim commentators on the Koran held that because Zaynab was from a higher class of society and her husband was only a freed slave, she could not tolerate living with him. She would always take pride in praising her own nobility, youth, and beauty, they claimed, and so insisted on divorce. The apologists also tell us that, as she was one of Muhammad's cousins, her husband could not have prevented her from seeking separation merely by refusing to give her a divorce, even though this is a man's absolute right in Islam.

Although there is no tangible proof to discredit the above rationalizations, the fact still remains that any dispute between Zayd and his wife intensified, if not actually started, on the very day Muhammad visited his daughter-in-law at her home alone.

After Zayd dissolved his marriage with Zaynab, another law was deemed necessary to sever the kinship relationship of Muhammad and his adopted son forever. This law was seriously needed to stop the criticism of those who saw in his act a shameful crime against the existing customs of the community. Accordingly, Allah sent the following command: "Muhammad is not the father of any man among you, but he is the messenger of Allah and the Seal of the Prophets." (Koran 33: 40)

> To calm down the scandalized clamor of the prophet's contemporaries, the Muslim God brought an innovation in adoption which was to influence until our days the institution in the Muslim world. Verse four of Sura XXXIII abolished adoption as an institution creating legal and affinal ties between individuals.[27]

Thus, the relationship of father and son between him and Zayd was rescinded. Instead, his former son is reminded that Muhammad holds the high position of messenger of Allah! Moreover, he is "the Seal of the Prophets," which means that he is the last prophet ordained by Allah to guide the people of Arabia on the new path of Islam. It also signified the fact that if the previous prophets had decreed the marriage of a father to his daughter-in-law to be unlawful, Muhammad can now make it allowable with Allah's blessing.

The expression "Seal of the Prophets" was first used by a Persian prophet named Manes. After introducing a new religion combining Zoroastrian duality and Christian soteriology, he called himself the seal or conclusion of prophets. After Manes preached in Babylonia, it is probable that the expression "Seal of the Prophets" spread to Arabia some four centuries before Muhammad, who very ingeniously used the phrase to make his followers believe that after him there would be no more prophets.

Aisha, Muhammad's favorite wife, narrated later that nothing was so detrimental to the Koran and Muhammad's image as the scandalous marriage of Zaynab, which was against all the prevailing customs. After Muhammad recited to Aisha the revelation in which Allah gave him the permission to marry Zaynab, his young wife, apparently feeling humiliated by having to share her husband with still another cowife, sarcastically told him, "Your Lord is very quick in answering your wish." Zaynab is the only one of Muhammad's wives who is mentioned by name in the Koran. She was always boastful that she was privileged by Allah to be named in the Muslim scripture. "Zaynab claimed a special glory as having been given by God to the prophet, whereas his other wives he had chosen for himself."[28]

Muhammad seemed to care much for Zayd, his freed slave, and later rewarded him for his devotion. He was appointed as the head of a small army on several expeditions, and it is reported by some exegetes that Muhammad intended to make him his own successor. Aisha is among those who held that Zayd was chosen as the successor to the Prophet. However, the ill-fated husband was killed in one of the forays against the tribes who were under the protection of the Byzantine Empire.

Another important outcome of this marriage between Muhammad and Zaynab was the law for veiling and seclusion. All the commentators on the Koran agree that Muhammad commanded women to wear veils at this time. "The seclusion and the veil as costume were at this time enjoined upon the wives of Muhammad."[29] Clearly the Zaynab episode led to this decree, which was designed to prevent other such episodes in the future. We shall be referring to the ordinance of the veil, with more details, in chapter 5.

THE SIEGE OF KHAYBAR:
THE CAPTIVE SAFIYYA
BECOMES MUHAMMAD'S WIFE

In the seventh year after the Hegira, Muhammad directed his men against another Jewish settlement in Arabia, which was called Khaybar (from the Hebrew word meaning "community"). Khaybar, located about a hundred miles north of Medina, was a rich and fertile land with "vast palm plantations in between plains of volcanic rocks."[30] The villages were scattered amid corn-fields and date palms.[31]

Muhammad's troops covered the distance in three days and on the fourth day surrounded the fortresses protecting Khaybar. The Jews had labored for many generations to plant date palms and improve the land for wheat, barley, and summer crops. The settlers were rich and in a much better position, as far as the living standard was concerned, than almost any other tribe in the northern and central parts of the Arabian Peninsula.

Seven very well fortified fortresses stood in different parts of the settlement. When news of the approaching Muslim army reached the Khaybar settlers, they hurriedly gathered their belongings and entered the citadel of al-Kamus. Muslims surrounded the fortress and inflicted heavy losses. After a month, the defenders of al-Kamus were allowed to surrender on one condition—the people must leave the country and give all of their property to the Muslims.[32]

Some accounts say the siege lasted two months. Ibn Ishaq, the biographer of Muhammad, provides us with the names of all the fortresses as well as their locations. Ninety male defenders fell and thereafter the chief of one of the fortresses, named Kinana, was brought to Muhammad, who demanded to know where he had hidden his treasures. The chief denied having any hidden hoard of goods, whereupon Muhammad ordered his men to force this information from Kinana and his cousin under physical torture.

They tied the hands and legs of the two men to wooden posts and as they lay prone a fire was lit upon their breasts. This cruel torture continued until they could bear it no longer and fainted. When Kinana and his cousin regained consciousness, Muhammad instructed his cousin Zubayr to kill them and sever their heads.

The booty of the forts was beyond Muslim expectations. The best part of the property was requested for "Allah" and Muhammad himself. Silverware, golden pots, armor, saddles, tents, horses, camels, sheep, goats, and everything else that was found in the fortresses were distributed among the Muslim invaders. Muhammad learned that Kinana, who was just tortured and killed, had recently married a young, beautiful girl with big black eyes.

He sent his servant Bilal, an African slave, to fetch the chief's bride. The huge slave found the woman, Safiyya, a girl of seventeen, and took her across the battlefield where she saw the corpses of her husband and his cousin, left with all the signs of the savagery and barbaric torture inflicted upon them. The poor woman was shivering with horror when she was presented to the conqueror. No sooner had Muhammad cast a glance

upon her than he was gripped with passion. He proposed Islam to her and forced her to "become the wife of
the murderer of her husband, her father, and her
brothers, of the treacherous enemy who had all but
exterminated her race."[33]

There was no other alternative except to keep her
faith and remain a slave, a concubine. Muhammad
threw his mantle over her shoulders, a sign in ancient
Arabia meaning that she belonged to him. (See chapter 5
on the veil and seclusion for more information.)

Incidentally, Safiyya means "tidbit," a specially
selected article from the spoils, which the chief chooses
for himself. The word can refer to a she-camel, horse,
sword, young woman, or girl. It is, therefore, possible
that the girl's real name was not Safiyya, and that this
surname might have been given to her by Muhammad,
who was in the habit of nicknaming all of his companions as well as his camel, furniture, and even his armor!

In any case, Safiyya was sent to Umm Sukim (the
mother of Muhammad's servant) to wash and dress her
for the wedding night. The founder of Islam celebrated
his wedding over the dead bodies of his adversaries and
consummated his marriage the very night that his bride's
late husband was beheaded by his order. In doing this
Muhammad seems to have broken a Koranic law. For a
Muslim male may not cohabit with a widow before a prescribed waiting period has expired. See Koran 2: 235:
"And do not consummate the marriage until [the term]
prescribed is run."

As a result of his successes on the battlefield, Muhammad had become exceedingly rich. In pre-Islamic
days, the chief would take one-fourth of the booty for

himself. In some parts of Arabia, the lion's share was one-fifth. Muhammad, through a special revelation, chose the latter portion (i.e., one-fifth) and promulgated this pagan rite as the law of Allah (Koran 8: 41). Thus, he was able to give to his wives and concubines enough silver and other ornamental articles to last them the rest of their lives. His daughters, friends, associates, and even their slaves all got rich.

The news of the raid and the fall of Khaybar was a warning to the people of the neighboring village of Fadak. They were quick to realize that it was best to capitulate and offer their village to the Muslim marauders before they came to seize it. This event also increased Muhammad's wealth.

For according to the Koran, any piece of land or booty which is acquired without the use of the sword belonged entirely to Muhammad. The village of Fadak, which surrendered unconditionally, became Muhammad's personal property and was later transferred to Fatima, his only living child. But Abu Bakr and 'Umar, his two fathers-in-law and successors, were just as greedy as their leader, and after his death they expropriated it completely.

MUHAMMAD REESTABLISHES HIS CONNECTIONS WITH MECCA THROUGH TWO STRATEGIC MARRIAGES: UMM HABIBA AND MAYMUNA

With the power and prestige he had acquired—Muhammad's name was now known all over the Arabian Peninsula—he was able to afford another wife. At this time, he married a woman named Umm Habiba, the widowed daughter of Abu Sufyan, his chief adversary in Mecca. The girl happened to live in Medina at the time and Muhammad thought that she could be useful as a key element in manipulating her father, an influential figure in Mecca from the house of Quraysh. He thus found it to his advantage to add yet one more wife to his crowded harem.

In the same year (the seventh after the Hegira), through a special agreement drawn up between him and the chieftains of Mecca, Muhammad was given permission to enter his former home town to make a pilgrimage to the Ka'aba. According to the terms of the contract, he could stay only three days, which was long enough for a man like him to arrange for a new marriage. He took advantage of this trip and married the sister of his uncle's wife, a twenty-seven-year-old widow named Maymuna. He intended to prolong his stay in order to consummate the marriage in Mecca, but the Qurayshite chiefs refused to extend the length of his visit. Muhammad's marriage with Maymuna was contracted with the help of his uncle, 'Abbas, who acted as her guardian. In fact, he was giving away his sister-in-law to his own nephew, Muhammad.

Muslim exegetes have had controversial discussions over the consummation of this marriage. Some argue that Muhammad must have remained abstinent because, according to a pagan rite, anyone who makes a pilgrimage to the Ka'aba must abstain from sexual intercourse. They therefore believe that he consummated this marriage in a place called Sarif, eight miles away from the town of Mecca. There are others who maintain that he was not abstinent and consummated the marriage while he was still in Mecca.

His uncle 'Abbas, the bride's guardian, was at that time a pagan, but he was also a brilliant tradesman and a sharp moneylender. He realized that the political power was definitely drifting from Mecca to Medina and his nephew by now was the absolute master of central Arabia. The family of 'Abbas benefited tremendously from their relationship with Muhammad. The marriage of 'Abbas's sister-in-law to the Prophet paved the way for this shrewd businessman to get as close as possible to the new source of power in Arabia. 'Abbas's great-grandson later originated the 'Abbasid Caliphate in Baghdad.[34]

In that same year Muhammad raided two more tribes, the Banu 'Amir and the Banu Melouh. At Hunain as the booty was being distributed, his followers began to riot as they thought that the spoils were not being divided equally. Apparently, they pushed the messenger of Allah aside (against a tree, according to some biographers) and rushed toward the captured plunder to get as large a share as possible. Muhammad tried to quiet them but to no avail. His clothes were torn in the melee and he was obliged to comply with the demands of the believers and divide all of the spoils, including female captives, equally among the greedy men of his boastful army. Evidently, this was the only time that Muhammad did not have first choice of the women, as was customary with him. But he did not forget to include his son-in-law in the division of the female captives.[35] The rough treatment of the Prophet by his own men shows that at this time many of his followers felt no particular reverence for Muhammad or his religion but were involved in his campaigns solely for their own self-interests.

THE CONQUEST OF MECCA: THREE PROSPECTIVE WIVES CHOOSE NOT TO JOIN HIS HAREM

The eighth year after the Hegira was of spectacular importance, both for Muhammad's life and for the future of Islam. In this year he conquered Mecca, his home town and the place where the pantheon of the pagan Arabs, the sanctuary of Ka'aba, was located. The sacred house of Allah, and originally of his three daughters, al-Lat, al-Uzza, and al-Manat, as well, would someday become the center of worship for all Muslims worldwide.

He entered triumphantly the very town from which he had had to flee in disguise some eight years before. After the ceremonial pilgrimage to Ka'aba, he stayed a few more days to make some changes in governorship and administration. His chief antagonist and also his brother-in-law, Abu Sufyan, conceded to the conqueror that his deity had been defended by Allah.[36] He thus expressed his willingness to embrace Islam.

The religious ceremonies performed by Muhammad on the day of the fall of Mecca were not in any way different from those that the pagans had long observed. The sanctity of the Ka'aba was preserved and the rites of the pilgrimage were maintained as in pre-Islamic days.[37] But a significant innovation was the destruction of the many idols representing the various deities of Mecca.

Allah became the supreme and only God; henceforth there would be no need for any others. Thus, Allah's rivals, the pre-Islamic gods and goddesses, which for many centuries had formed the core of Arabian mythology, were annihilated. Muhammad's childhood god, Allah, was now recognized as the only God.

The new converts gathered around Muhammad. By shaking the Prophet's hand, the men vowed allegiance to Allah's apostle. The women converts were not allowed to shake his hand (*Bai'at* in Arabic).

After appointing some of his men as the mayor and religious jurists of the town, Muhammad turned his mind, as usual, to another wife. He chose a woman named 'Asma Bint al-Numan, but on the wedding night she stubbornly refused to submit to his sexual desires. Ibn Sa'ad, one of the earliest chronologists, tells the story this way:

> When she ['Asma Bint al-Numan] entered the room where he [the Prophet] was, he closed the door and released the curtain. When he thrust his hands toward her, she said, "I take refuge in Allah from thee." The

prophet immediately covered his head with his sleeve
and said, "You are granted such a protection."[38]

According to some of the biographers, the new bride
was not only very conceited and took pride in her birth
and house, but she was full of hatred for the man who
had spilled so much blood in many clans. Another account of the wedding night describes 'Asma as asking
Muhammad: "Should a queen give herself to one of the
people? I come from a tribe which receives everything
and gives nothing. I ask God to protect me against you."[39]

It is maintained by some of the earliest exegetes that
'Asma was a young, charming woman from a famous
and well-to-do clan. Muhammad was in his early sixties,
with a harem full of young, lovely wives. "She hated to
share the same man with all the others, and Muhammad's power and money were not a strong motive
for her to make him desirable."[40] Al-Bukhari explains
that she rejected him simply because she did not like
him.[41] Whatever happened, Muhammad repudiated
'Asma that same evening and sent her to her folks.

Muhammad encountered similar refusals from two
other Meccan women he wished to add to his harem.
One, named Mulayka, is described by some early historians as hysterical.[42] Others maintain that she was young
and charming but simply did not care to sleep with
Muhammad.[43] Still others hold that the separation was
due to "symptoms of illness resembling leprosy."[44]

Finally, the other woman who declined to cohabit
with Allah's messenger on her wedding night was
named Fatima, the daughter of 'Abd Duhhak.[45]

By this time Muhammad's second wife, Sauda, was

entering her forties (he was sixty). Having many young, pretty wives in his harem, he decided to divorce Sauda. Since she had been led to believe that the door of paradise would be open to all women who had shared the messenger's bed, she pleaded desperately with him not to divorce her. She wanted to be counted among the wives of Allah's Prophet on the day of resurrection.

Muhammad allowed her to stay on one condition: that she forgo any future sexual intercourse with him. She agreed and remained as his wife, giving all of her own rights to sexual intercourse with her husband over to Aisha, her cowife and Muhammad's favorite.*

THE AFFAIR WITH MARIYA, THE COPTIC CONCUBINE

The scandals of Muhammad's sexual affairs reached a climax as the result of an incident that took place in the home of Hafsa, one of his wives. Muhammad had provided a separate house for each of his wives, all of which were in close proximity. He divided his time among his wives, giving each her due sexually, although he still preferred Aisha and Zaynab most.

One day when Muhammad came to Hafsa's house, he found that the woman was out visiting her father. While still there, his Coptic concubine, Mariya, arrived;

---

*According to the Koran, a man with more than one wife must divide his time equally among them. Each wife is entitled to the right of sexual intercourse on an equal basis. Concubines are allowed only half of the cohabitation rights of legal wives.

she had been presented to Muhammad by the governor of Alexandria some time ago. The Prophet, evidently overcome with desire, could not resist the temptation of making love with the pretty-faced young woman right then and there. It is recorded that her "skin was white and tender." In the middle of their love-making the door opened and in came his wife Hafsa. "He was caught by one of his wives, Hafsa, the proud daughter of his companion, 'Umar, having intercourse with Mariya in Hafsa's own room and on her own day."[46]

She raised her voice against the unfaithful husband, who left the bed immediately and pulled himself together. "In my house, in my bed, and on my own day!" she burst out in anger. The charming Coptic girl, Mariya, left the room in embarrassment, while Muhammad tried to quiet his wife, who was enraged beyond all expectation.

Eventually, he succeeded in calming her down by promising not to touch Mariya any more. He took an oath vowing from that moment on not to have intercourse with Mariya. In return for such a solemn promise of fidelity, Muhammad asked his wife to keep the incident to herself. But this sort of scandal, probably unprecedented in the life history of any prophet, was not something that could be hushed up so easily. As soon as her husband left the house, Hafsa went up to Aisha, her cowife and close friend, and related the entire story, adding emphatically that Muhammad had promised not to have sexual relations with the charming concubine anymore.

It was reported by virtually all the Muslim chronologists that the Coptic girl bore a son by Muhammad, "his fatherhood being attested by the infant's features."[47] The child caused much concern and jealousy among the legal wives, who could not procure any issue for Muhammad, because they thought the Prophet's legacy and his title would be transferred to this male descendent and the dynasty would be perpetuated by him. Aisha, Muhammad's favorite wife, was extremely jealous, as she too was childless. Indeed, she was so envious that she even denied any resemblance between the child and his father.

As it turned out, the child died in infancy, which caused deep sorrow for the alleged father, but brought relief to the wives of the harem. Did the child really belong to Muhammad? It is not certain, and the lack of resemblance, according to Aisha, affirms our doubt, especially when reliable biographers state that the fidelity of the slave girl was questionable, as will be shown shortly. On the other hand, we know that none of his wives, who numbered more than ten and all of whom were young, could bear him children. Furthermore, Muhammad was already the father of six children from his first wife, Khadija, all but one of whom died in his lifetime. Perhaps the intense jealousy among his wives can be explained by the assumption that the pretty concubine was indeed able to bear him a male child, who, had he survived, would probably have become heir to the desert throne.

The attractive handmaiden had an overwhelming power over Muhammad to such a degree that even Aisha, the teenaged queen of the harem, was extremely jealous of her, and this hatred is best illustrated in Aisha's own words: "I was never so jealous as I was with Mariya, that is because she was a very beautiful curly-haired woman. The prophet was very attracted to her."[48]

For Muhammad, it was a double deprivation. First, his wives, especially Aisha and Hafsa, refused to have any sexual intercourse with him after he was caught in his wife's bed with Mariya, and second, to stay away from the curly-haired maiden was more easily said than done. Lack of sexual satisfaction for a man of his appetites was difficult and eventually he broke his vow and resumed seeing the slave girl. He even went so far as to move into Mariya's apartment, despite his solemn promise and his wives' objections.

But breaking a solemn promise and disregarding a vow were considered very loathsome and, in fact, degrading acts to the Arabs. Muhammad needed some divine sanction to quiet the protests of his followers— notably his wives. Allah had never failed to come to the aid of his messenger when the need was felt, and, as usual, the following verse was revealed: "O Prophet! Why bannest thou that which Allah hath made lawful for thee, seeking to please thy wives?" (Koran 66: 1) Thus, Muhammad broke his vow with the sanction of Allah.

In commenting about the foregoing passage of the Koran, some of the exegetes tried desperately to save Muhammad's name from the shameful act he committed in his wife's bed in her absence. They have fabricated a childish story to justify Muhammad's breaking of the solemn promise which is reflected in Sura 66 of the Koran.

They argue that it was honey, not the Coptic girl, that Muhammad vowed not to touch anymore! The fabricated story goes as follows:

The Prophet was very fond of honey. One of his wives received a present of honey from a relative and by its means inveigled the Prophet into staying with her longer than was customary. The others felt aggrieved, and Ayeshah [Aisha] devised a little plot. Knowing the Prophet's horror of unpleasant smells, she arranged with two other wives that they should hold their noses when he came to them after eating the honey, and accuse him of having eaten the produce of a very rank-smelling tree. When they accused him of having eaten *Maghâfîr* [a strong-smelling herb] the Prophet said that he had eaten only honey. They said: "The bees had fed on Maghâfîr." The Prophet was dismayed and vowed to eat no more honey.[49]

It is hard to believe that anyone with average intelligence could be so naive as to accept such a ridiculous story. At least five reasons can be mentioned for rejecting its authenticity:

1. If Muhammad was so easily tempted by honey to stay longer in any one of his wives' houses, then the other rival cowives could have provided the same enticement and lured him back.

2. If Muhammad had stayed with one of his wives longer than was her due, then he would have acted against the ordinance of the Koran, which explicitly decrees that the polygamous husband must treat his wives with equality as far as affection and sexual intercourse are concerned.

3. Even the orthodox exegete Pickthall, whose translation of the Koran is quoted above, admits that "The commentators generally prefer (2) [i.e., the Mariya/Hafsa tale] as more explanatory of the text."[50]

4. The most reliable document in this episode is the Koran itself, which clearly refers to the story of Hafsa and

Aisha in the next four verses. Thus, the first verse of Sura 66, quoted above, is closely connected to the other following verses and there is no doubt that Muhammad, out of embarrassment, was obliged to promise not to touch his concubine anymore in order to stop the scandal.

5. If we accept the childish and ridiculous story of Muhammad promising his wives not to eat honey, then those wives who plotted against him by holding their noses from his bad breath are simply liars who deceived their husband and are not worthy of becoming "the mothers of all the believers," a title given to them by Allah in the Koran. Moreover, the house of Muhammad is reduced to a center of intrigue and conspiracy, to which no Muslim believer would be willing to admit.

It seems more likely that Muhammad had decided to arouse the jealousy of Aisha and Hafsa by going directly to Mariya's quarters and spending an entire month with her. This tactic did not work, however, and he could not gain back the affection of his humiliated wives as before. Consequently, Muhammad fell into a state of depression until he was visited by Hafsa's father, 'Umar. Asking the reason for his discomfort, the Prophet told 'Umar that his two favorite wives did not care for him any more. 'Umar, who was noted for his frankness and sharp mind, responded, "We others of Quraysh, we know how to control our women. But, we have come among people [the Medinans] where it is the women who are in control."[51]

Muhammad got the message. He knew he must shake the big stick; soft words had not paid off. He concluded that he should refer his domestic situation to Allah, who once more brought forth the solution, in the form of a revelation:

If ye twain [Hafsa and Aisha] turn unto Allah repen-
tant, for your hearts desired [the ban]; and if ye aid
one another against him [Muhammad] then lo! Allah,
even he, is his protecting Friend and Gabriel and the
righteous among the believers; and furthermore the
angels are his helpers. (Koran 66: 4)

Here Allah admonished Hafsa and Aisha to repent
and refrain from helping each other against Muhammad, because Allah, his angels, and the good people
among the Muslims would protect the apostle from their
guile. An objective person, reading this passage, must
ask, What were Aisha and Hafsa doing which necessitated a harsh warning from Allah? Clearly nothing
whatsoever, except that they did not want to share their
beds with a man who would take a slave girl into the
bed of a legal wife. They thought that they had been
debased.

Beside the unfairness of the above Koranic passage,
it is somewhat ridiculous to think that the supreme deity
would take a personal interest in the sex life of his
Prophet. Nonetheless, Islamic libraries are filled with
volumes about the sexual practices of married couples in
a religious context. For example: "The coital embrace is
surrounded by a ceremony which grants Allah a substantial presence in the man's mind during coitus."[52]

Despite Allah's harsh warning, his favorite teenaged
wife, Aisha, was as determined as ever to stay away
from him. Her friend and cowife did the same thing;
both of them still refused Muhammad's sexual
advances. So, upon the advice of his companion, 'Umar,
Muhammad became more stern and threatened them

with divorce. The result of this new plan was the following revelation: "It may happen that his Lord, if he
divorce you, will give him in your stead wives better
than you, submissive, believing, pious, penitent, in-
clined to fasting, widows and virgins." (Koran 66: 5)

The threat to divorce Hafsa and Aisha and replace
them with new wives was not something that the two
young women could take lightly. If they continued their
bed strike, they could end up as outcasts from society.
Muhammad was rich, powerful, and above all, he was
the religious leader of a force of people who would do
anything to please him. The men would even divorce
their wives so that he might marry them. Muhammad's
wives knew that many other Muslim women would be
more than willing to become the Prophet's wife. They
were aware that by a special ordinance Muhammad was
permitted to have as many wives as his heart pleased.

The above-quoted verse from the Koran (66: 5) tells
us something that most of the exegetes have not paid
attention to, or in some instances have deliberately over-
looked. The verse reveals how Muhammad felt about
women and what he really wanted from them. To him, a
wife is ideal only when she is submissive. A wife's submission to her husband is the first rule in Islamic
jurisprudence. In the eyes of the founder of Islam, subjugation of the wife is even more important than creed.
That is why in the above verse, submission is mentioned
prior to believing. He wants his wives to be obedient to
him, to follow his instructions whatever they may be.
We shall later see how this doctrine has infiltrated the
minds and hearts of millions of Muslim males all over
the world.

Fasting is also important for a wife because it means a frugal, thrifty, and sparing mate. She must get used to the idea of being deprived of food if need be and fasting teaches her just that. She must also be penitent, one who repents of sins. A major sin for woman is disobedience and if she is not submissive, she must repent. In short, the ideal wife for Allah's apostle is literally nothing more than a female slave.

This sort of mentality and attitude toward the women is apparent not only in this one verse but all throughout the Koran and in Muhammad's own words and deeds, as related by tradition.

Although Muhammad had succeeded in intimidating his wives, he realized he needed to be more cautious in regard to Mariya. He therefore found a place for his concubine in the upper-class quarters of Medina, away from all of his wives and their extreme jealousy. According to Aisha, "At the beginning, she was living near us and the prophet spent entire days and nights with her until we protested and she became frightened."[53]

But problems persisted. Muhammad had assigned a Coptic male servant to Mariya to do her necessary daily work. Soon a rumor spread across town that the charming concubine, who lived all by herself in a separate house, was having an affair with this male attendant. The rumor was so strongly voiced that Muhammad could not disregard it for long. He instructed his cousin 'Ali to investigate the charges against Mariya's infidelity. When 'Ali arrived at Mariya's house, her servant was in the act of climbing a palm tree. 'Ali drew his sword, shouted, and threatened the man, who, taken by surprise, slid down the tree in terror. Because the early

Arabs, like most bedouins today, were not in the habit of wearing underpants, 'Ali unintentionally saw the man's private parts as he slid down the tree. The occasion revealed a secret: the servant was a eunuch.[54]

Though we cannot totally rule out the possibility that the male servant was a eunuch, Islamic historians are unable to present proof that Mariya's attendant was indeed impotent. The story seems too artless to be true. Why did 'Ali, whose mission was merely to investigate the allegation, threaten the slave with a drawn sword? Why would the slave, who should have been certain of his own innocence, slide down to the ground in terror? The details of the story don't ring true. When a man climbs a palm tree, his back is toward the outside. How then could 'Ali have seen that he was a eunuch? It would have been quite natural for a young, charming girl like Mariya, who was secluded in her quarters and was not permitted to see any man except her master every twenty days or so, to develop a relationship with a man who was her regular contact with the outside world and who spoke the same language (Coptic). He was also a slave like herself, was much younger than her master, and had been her companion since they had left Egypt together to be presented to Muhammad as good will gifts.

But, on the other hand, in a harem, intrigue, conspiracy, and especially jealousy were not uncommon, so much so that sometimes bloody feuds broke out among those concerned. It is therefore possible that the infidelity of the girl was fabricated or suggested by Aisha out of extreme jealousy and spread around by her cowives.

This was not the first time that the faithfulness of one

of Muhammad's wives was in doubt. Some three or four years prior to the Mariya incident, a rumor of Aisha's infidelity was the topic of the day.

According to Islamic tradition, on one of Muhammad's expeditions, Aisha left camp one night during a halt, "to answer the call of nature." When she came back, she noticed that her necklace was missing. She hurried back to look for it but by the time she returned the caravan had departed.

A soldier was ordered to follow the caravan and pick up anything that might have been left behind. He quickly caught up with Aisha and offered her his own camel. They managed to reach the caravan the next day, but her absence from the camp during the entire night and her appearance the next day in the company of a young, handsome camel driver was enough to spread rumors of her infidelity among the believers.

The irony is that the two members of Muhammad's harem who were subjected to these allegations had almost the same qualities: both of them were very young (in their teens), both were reported to be beautiful and charming, and both were Muhammad's favorites. It would not be surprising if both were also unfaithful. Sharing an old man with many other cowives must have taken its toll, regardless of the position and status of the husband.

MUHAMMAD'S CONCEPTION OF PARADISE: A PRIMITIVE MALE FANTASY

The foregoing section should have made it clear that Muhammad's sexual drive was relentless, and it is for this reason that he enjoyed a harem full of young wives as well as a favorite concubine. We have seen that women were often considered the spoils of war and they were treated as prize possessions by the male warriors in Muhammad's entourage. These male-biased attitudes heavily influenced the development of Muslim religious ideas, and nowhere is this more obvious than in Muhammad's conception of the afterlife. According to the Koran, the male who is submissive to Allah and to his Prophet will be granted a paradise of many beautiful maidens for his personal pleasure throughout eternity!

These heavenly damsels of great beauty and eternal youth are called "houris," which literally means, "girls with big, black eyes." The word *hur* ("nymph") is used four times in the Koran (52: 20; 56: 22; 55: 72; and 44: 54). The houris have special qualities in which the Arab male is most interested: they don't sleep, perspire, get pregnant, menstruate, or ever become ill! Each of the male believers who enters "paradise" is rewarded with at least seventy of these heavenly nymphs, plus all of his own earthly wives.

Clearly, Muhammad's promised heaven was envisaged mostly with the male believer in mind and is described in the Koran as follows:

And for those who feareth the tribunal of his lord, there are two gardens ... dowered with branches. In each of them two fountains flow. ... In each of them there are of every fruit two kinds. ... They [the male believers] recline upon couches of which the inner lining is of brocade and the fruits of the two gardens hang low. ... In them are maidens restraining in their glances, whom neither man nor demon hath approached before them. ... [In beauty] like the jacynth and the coralstones. (Koran 55: 46, 48, 50, 52, 54, 56, 58)

The Koran continues:

And besides these two, there are two other gardens, ... dark green. ... In each of them are two fountains, flowing abundantly. ... In each are maidens, good, beauteous Houris, enclosed in Pavilions, ... whom neither man nor demon hath approached before them. ... [The just] recline on green pillows and beautiful carpets. (Koran 55: 62, 64, 66, 68, 70, 72, 74, 76)

This description of paradise, revealed in Mecca, reflects Muhammad's early need to call to his new faith as many people as possible. He offers them encouragement by promising them a garden paradise. It also reflects his own wishful thinking, a fantasy of perfection in living that any typical male Arab bedouin of that time might desire. Let us look at the details.

Two Fountains Flow

Muhammad spent fifty-three years of his life in Mecca, which is located in the middle of a desert, surrounded by hot, rocky hills and vast stretches of sand. Mecca has no river, trees, fountains, or fruits. The heat is intense during the daytime. Therefore, a green spot with a little rainwater is a blessing to anyone living in such primitive, miserable conditions. The oasis with a pond of rainwater and a few palm trees is the most important of gifts from nature for desert wanderers.

Muhammad, like most of his home-town people, had never tasted the fresh, cool waters of an underground spring or a brook rushing down from the heights of snow-covered mountains. Nothing but the brackish waters of the desert wells or ponds quenches the thirst of desert people, especially in the hot season. The sight of a river, stream, or even a brook with flowing, fresh water would be a gift beyond all expectation. Since Muhammad knew he could never have the blessings of fresh, running waters of big rivers in this world, he promised his followers not one but two gardens in the next world: "In each of them [the gardens] two fountains flow."

The Heavenly Oasis

Mecca is very hot, especially in spring and summer. The sunshine reflects off the rocks and sands, making it quite unbearable. There are no trees or greenery because of the heat, lack of water, and poor soil conditions. What would be more inviting to an Arab in a hot, blazing desert than dense, green trees providing cool shade where one can relax from the intense heat and blinding sun? Therefore, paradise consists of "two gardens dowered with branches."

For the very reason mentioned above, no fruit is grown in Mecca; it has to be imported from distant towns. Since the only means of transportation in those days was camels or donkeys, very little fresh fruit except perhaps dates would reach the town. Thus, Muhammad's promised paradise is rich with fruit trees. "In each of them are fruits and dates and pomegranates." (Koran 55: 68)

The many other varieties of fruits are unknown to Muhammad. His knowledge was limited to the few trees available in his neighborhood and so is his paradise.

The date, however, is a main source of nourishment in that part of the world. Climbing a thorny, high palm tree, both at the time of cross-pollination and immediately after the dates are ready to be picked, is very difficult and cumbersome indeed. Only expert date-pickers could do that efficiently. In Muhammad's paradise, however, the pious believers do not have to worry about climbing such awkward trees because the fruits of all the trees are at reach and near at hand: "The fruits of two gardens hang low."

Wine Aplenty

The pre-Islamic Arab was fond of wine. Arabian literature before Islam comprises a good deal of poetry and proverbs praising wine. Muhammad's uncle Hamza was a heavy wine drinker even after he embraced Islam. The story is told that one day he became inebriated and killed two camels, which were 'Ali's share of the spoils from Badr (a place where the Muslims had battled their enemies). When Muhammad protested, Hamza snapped back with contempt, "Were you not once the slave of my father?" It was after this incident that Muhammad prohibited wine drinking. But one cannot destroy an old custom merely with a verse of scripture. The ancient Arabs appreciated wine, and there were a number of wine sellers in Mecca who would also provide female companionship for their patrons. In order to deprive Arabs of wine drinking in this world, Muhammad had to promise a better wine in paradise. A garden with black-eyed maidens, reclining couches, fruits, and other comforts would not be complete without wine!

Thus, wine drinking would be permitted in paradise and this heavenly wine would produce no hangover! How did Muhammad know about the headache resulting from the overdrinking of wine? We have enough evidence to show that before his exile in Medina he was an occasional, if not a regular, visitor to the wine sellers' shops in Mecca. It is possible that most of the stories about the ancient Jewish prophets related in the Koran were heard from the regular visitors of the taverns. It is narrated in one of the traditions about his life that Muhammad confessed on two occasions that when he was grazing the flocks in his childhood, he "left the care of the beasts to one of his companions in order to take part in the revelries of the town."[55]

Early biographers also state that Muhammad drank wine on occasion and continued this practice up to the battle of Uhud.[56] Others hold that he stopped drinking wine four months before the battle.[57] In fact, the restrictions placed on drinking alcoholic beverages was gradual. For instance, on one occasion his followers asked him about the drinking of wine and gambling.

The response was ambiguous: "They question thee about strong drink and games of chance. Say: In both is great sin, and utility for men; but the sin of them is greater than their usefulness." (Koran 2: 219)

After this, the Prophet noticed that when his followers were drunk, they did not follow the rules in praying and didn't know how to perform the religious rites. As a result, he told them that whenever they were drunk, "don't draw near unto prayer until you know that which you utter." (Koran 4: 43)

The above revelation was made at the end of the third year of his flight to Medina, which means at least sixteen years after the beginning of his prophetic career. Thus, drinking must have been prevalent among his followers up to the end of the third year of the Hegira and it should be no surprise if the Prophet of Allah drank wine and had experienced hangovers.

At first the proscription against wine drinking met with powerful resistance. The pagan Arabs were used to drinking and the community was not ready to give it all up so easily. Ibn Sa'ad has narrated that the Prophet himself used to drink *nabidh,* which is a sort of wine.[58] As was pointed out, Muhammad's uncle Hamza was a very heavy drinker. He is reported to have been drunk in the battle of Uhud, which took place between Muslims and the Qurayshites near Medina. Hamza was killed by a slave lancer whose owner, Hant, a woman from Mecca and the Prophet's adversary, promised his freedom for eliminating Muhammad's uncle. Once the killing was done, the slave was freed by Hant. Muhammad prohibited hard drinking after this battle, perhaps as a result of Hamza's death.

Red wine, of course, goes very well with the white meat of fowls, which is so generously promised in the next world. Muhammad must have heard about the customs of Persian and Byzantine courtiers, and like most Arabs of his day, he wanted to experience the luxury of being opulent and powerful like the emperors of the neighboring countries. Reclining on curtained and decorated thrones while handsome youths served cups of wine, eating fruits and the well-prepared foods from the flesh of birds, and enjoying the companionship of beautiful girls, these were fantasies that he envisioned. Since it was impossible to provide these luxuries for his followers in a country as poor and barren as Arabia, he would most certainly promise them in his heaven:

> Those are they who will be brought nigh, in gardens of delight; a multitude of those of old and a few of those of later time, on lined couches, reclining therein face to face. There wait on them immortal youths, with bowls and ewers and a cup of a pure wine, wherefrom they get no aching of the head, nor any madness, and fruit that they prefer, and flesh from the fowls that they desire. (Koran 56: 11–21)

Women as the Ultimate Reward

Muhammad was very generous in giving away captured young women to his male followers. It has already been shown how, after he successfully raided a tribe, he divided the women prisoners up, married or single, among his followers. If the possession of captive women was a great incentive for the Arabs to join him in his new mission, the promise of the generous rewards of women to his male believers in the next world was also certainly a motivation. He was, as a consequence, very liberal with his promises about the number of female beauties that each man would enjoy in paradise.

Aside from what is said in the Koran about paradise, there are commentaries on the Koran that provide additional details of the afterlife. Each Muslim male in paradise will supposedly have the sexual potency of eighty men.[59] Furthermore, in this life, Muhammad, through a special dish prepared for him by the Archangel Gabriel, had acquired the potency of thirty men![60] For the nomadic Arabs of the seventh century, the strength of a man was not related to his intelligence, knowledge, or wisdom. Rather, he was evaluated by his sexual potency. The Arabs would accept a man as their leader when he could demonstrate his ability to handle large numbers of women. Thus, Muhammad, who was their leader in every respect, was expected to have a higher sexual potency than the average man.

> It is firmly established that in the matter of cohabitation, that Excellency [meaning Muhammad] had the power of thirty strong men given him. Therefore, it was lawful for that prince to take as many wives as he pleased, be they nine or more.[61]

In summary, Muhammad's paradise is everything that a nomadic Arab male of that time desired: an eternity of eating choice foods, drinking the best wines, and sexual intercourse with beautiful young women. Conspicuously absent in this depiction are any of the higher pleasures of life: art, music, the pursuit of knowledge, or the experience of love above the level of sexual desire. Muhammad seemed to know nothing of the love of lasting commitments, the love of friends, of children, of a devoted husband and wife.

What attraction would such a paradise be to women? Muhammad's heaven is just a projection of the Koranic tenets that restrict women's lives on earth. In both realms women are subjected to malicious discrimination. In the whole text of the Koran, there is not one verse to show that women will be treated equally in paradise. The sexuality of man is recognized, sanctioned, and amply provided for by the Muslim scripture, but the needs of women are totally left out. Although some of the descriptions of paradise mention "immortal youths," who serve wine to the husbands, there is no implication that women are given the same sexual freedom with these youths as the men are allowed with the houris. Women in paradise must be as faithful to their husbands as they were in their earthly existence. Wives must be submissive, subordinate, veiled, and secluded in the harems of heaven, watching quietly as their husbands make love with the beautiful houris of paradise. Man is her master on earth, and she will be subjugated to him forever in heaven as well.

Muhammad's control over his own wives continued even after his death, for he realized that if he did not issue a proscription, one or more of his younger followers would be able to marry his wives after his death. In his late fifties, with possibly a dozen young, charming wives in his harem, he must have occasionally wondered who would possess his beloved Aisha, and who would buy his Coptic slave girl, Mariya, and add her to his harem. There were rumors that some of his close followers wished him dead so that they might have access to his young wives. Zubayr, his cousin and close companion, is reported to have said that he was waiting for the old man, meaning Muhammad, to die, so that he might marry some of his wives.

Therefore, to quell these worries the following ingenious passage was revealed: "The Prophet is closer to the believers than themselves, and his wives are their mothers." (Koran 33: 6) With this decree from Allah, his wives were designated the mothers of all believers. Naturally, because of the incest taboo, no Muslim would think of marrying his mother!

There is no doubt that his extreme jealousy was the main reason for the above revelation, and it is also clear that the quoted passage is a reflection of his inner anxieties.

A peculiar feature of the above verse is that it clearly contradicts the previous passage which states: "Nor had he [Allah] made your wives your mothers." (Koran 33: 4) This is a reference to the pre-Islamic custom, according to which a man could divorce his wife by stating that her back appeared to him as his mother's back. Muhammad in 33: 4 is rescinding this ancient practice. Yet in 33: 6, he designates his own wives as the mothers of all believers. The two verses are certainly contradictory.

With the help of the verse 33: 6, Muhammad assured himself that no man would marry his wives after he was gone. But he had to be equally sure that his wives would not have love affairs with anyone else, nonbelievers, pagans, Christians, etc. For this reason he declared:

"And whosoever of you [meaning his wives] is submissive unto Allah and his messenger and doeth right, we shall give her reward twice over, and we have prepared for her a noble provision." (Koran 33: 31)

Thus, he placed a taboo on his wives to keep other men away from them and also gave them an incentive in the next life to remain faithful to him after his passing. He left behind him a legacy of male domination and control over woman, which has ensured her inferior status in Muslim society to this day. In the following chapters we will examine the maze of laws developed by Islamic jurisprudence to keep women subordinate.

2

PRIMITIVE MARRIAGE LAWS

The Arabic word for marriage is *nikah,* which, according to many Koranic commentators and Muslim jurists, means "unity."[1] This word, which occurs frequently in the Koran, is an old Semitic term that also means sexual intercourse.[2]

The Koran uses many "anatomical" words, derived from the names of the body parts of both animals and humans, the true meaning of which would surely offend a person of modest sensibilities. It was very common among pre-Islamic Arab poets to use phrases praising the reproductive organs: "It was not unusual in poems for a woman to extol the charms of her vagina, nor for a man to sing the praises of his penis."[3] Gradually, these words spread and developed new meanings. It is therefore not surprising to find out that the word used in the

Koran for marriage means sexual intercourse, not wedlock, as interpreted by various jurists.

The women of the pre-Islamic era were much freer in
their movements than they were subsequently allowed
to be. They showed hospitality to their husband's
friends.[4] They were regarded as equals to their men[5] and
their companionship was sought by men of all ranks.
Women attended public gatherings, took part in the
armed campaigns against the enemy, nursed the
wounded, encouraged the warriors by reciting verses of
songs and lyric poems, and held high offices.

The great majority of Arab women were nomads,
and this group enjoyed more freedom than urban females, who, under certain circumstances, were made to
observe some rules. Nomadic women were free to
mingle with men, work with them, milk and graze the
cattle, receive men in their tents, and dismiss them when
they pleased. Pre-Islamic women could even choose
their own mates.[6] In case of need, they could rely on
their tribes for help. They were indeed an asset to the
tribes and valuable members of their clans.

As for other, neighboring countries which were later
overrun by the Muslims, it is certain that the women of
these countries enjoyed a much happier life than what
was imposed upon them by Islam later on. The following pages will show, very briefly, the position held
by women in some of these countries prior to the advent
of Islam.

WOMEN IN ANCIENT EGYPT

The position of women in the Nile Valley before the Muslim raids was very favorable. A woman could initiate a courtship freely with a man, and if she wanted to, propose to the man of her choice. If the conjugal life proved impossible, she had the right to divorce her husband. She also had the right to draw up the terms of the marriage contract.

The Egyptian woman was unveiled and could move about freely at public gatherings without fear of prosecution. She attended to her own business affairs and was free to make trips or stay out of her home town visiting her relatives, a fact easily verified by the many letters that exist in the early Egyptian histories.

Some researchers maintain that women in pre-Islamic Egypt were in a much better position than many contemporary females in the advanced world. "The position of women," wrote Will Durant, "was more advanced than in most countries today. No people, ancient or modern, has given woman so high a legal status as did inhabitants of the Nile Valley."[7]

Many Egyptian women attained the highest political status—some became queens of that vast empire. Hatshepsut and Cleopatra are but two shining examples that illustrate the level of political achievement attained by Egyptian women in antiquity. These women ruled their country as well as many other male rulers before them, if not more efficiently and firmly, and they went to war or maintained the peace with the same zeal and willpower as their male counterparts.

The powerful pharaohs were very careful not to offend their wives. They respected them and admonished
their sons to treat their wives as nicely. "Make glad her
heart," instructed a pharaoh to his son, "during the time
thou hast her, for she is a field profitable to its owner. . . .
If thou oppose her it will mean thy ruin."[8] The pharaoh's
instruction directly contrasts with Allah's ordinance that
says, "Your women are (like) a tilled field for you, so go
into your tilled field as you will." (Koran 2: 223) According to the Koran, the wife's consent is not important.

In fact, ancient Egyptian women enjoyed so much
freedom that travelers to Egypt were often astonished at
such liberty. In marriage contracts, the obedience of the
husband was explicitly required. Diodorus Siculus, a
Greek writer, told exactly how the obedience of the husband was specified in marriage bonds.[9] A wife managed
her husband's property and supervised his estate. In
fact, she was the lord of the house. The servants and
slaves took their orders from her. "The woman in ancient Egypt was the full mistress of the house. She could
manage her husband's property and earnings, and
moreover, the estate descended in a female line."[10] The
surviving papyri show no divorce in ancient Egypt.

WOMEN IN BABYLONIA

The position of the woman in ancient Babylonia, though
not as high as in Egypt, was far superior to what Islam
has provided in the last fourteen centuries. Babylonian
women enjoyed a special independence that was unique
and unparalleled.

Protection of women's rights in Babylonia was one of the most outstanding achievements of the ancient world. According to the Code of Hammurabi, the man was responsible for the maintenance of his wife. He could not dismiss her even if she were incapable of carrying out the household duties. If her husband abandoned her willfully and left the town, a Babylonian woman had the right to marry another man of her choice; if her first husband returned, he had no right over her any more.

The guardianship of the children resided with the mother, and if she separated from her husband, he had to provide for their livelihood and subsistence. Upon her husband's death, she acquired a portion of his estates. "The married woman had a right to do business independently and most of the transactions were done by the women."[11]

We shall see later in more detail that even though some of the Islamic laws can be traced back to Babylonian and Assyrian prototypes, the ancient laws of these two great countries of the past were much more progressive than some Islamic laws even as they exist today.

WOMEN IN ELAM*

On the basis of many archeological discoveries obtained from the ancient city of Susa, we are certain that women in Elam had acquired a very high position in their so-

---

*An ancient kingdom in what is today the province of Khuzistan in southwestern Iran. It existed as a cultural and political entity as early as the fourth millennium B.C.E. and lasted until the seventh century B.C.E., when it was subsumed into the emerging Persian Empire.

ciety and were treated equally with men, some two thousand years before our era.[12]

Ancient cuneiform tablets reveal that the women of Elam could go to the courts, give their testimonies free of any formalities or restrictions, and they could file claims or defend their rights. In signing a contract, the nail print of the woman was placed next to that of her male counterpart. In one of these documents, we see that a man left all of his estates and properties to his only married daughter. In another, a father left his field to his daughter, and she, too, transferred the entire estate to her own daughter. In another document, a mother with two sons and a daughter bequeathed all of her estates solely to her daughter, and her two sons had to swear before the king that they would not file any claim against their mother's will.

Men in Elam had a great respect toward women and in many fields women enjoyed special privileges. According to one of the tablets, a man had stated that as long as he lived, his daughter would nurse him and after he was gone, she would be in charge of the preparation of sacrifices, alms giving, and the temple services. If any of his sons raised "any objections to the validity or contents of the will, his tongue and hand must be cut, and he ought to pay a fine equal to four minah" (one minah equalled sixty shekels). Of the sixteen witnesses who signed the testament, four were women.

One of the Elamite women became the ruler and absolute monarch of Susa. She was the sister of Shil-khakha, the grandmother of the great dynasty of Elam.

WOMEN OF INDIA

One of the Indian codes states: "The mother exceedeth a thousand fathers in the right of reverence."[13] The ancient people of India respected women and never dreamed of irritating a female. "The women are not to be struck even with a flower."[14]

From the different texts of ancient Indian literature, one can clearly infer that the women of India enjoyed much freedom in choosing their own husbands or in attending social gatherings. In religious rites or ceremonies, they were on equal standing with men. "She had more to say in choice of her mate than the forms of marriage might suggest. She appeared freely at feasts and dances, and joined with men in religious sacrifices."[15]

In part of India that fell under Muslim domination, the marriage laws were changed and Islamic rites replaced all of the previous social and religious customs. Women were barred from social gatherings. Singing, dancing, and mingling of the sexes were totally prohibited. Women were confined to their quarters and gradually lost their identities and privileges. They had to accept the veil, a practice that had been totally unknown previously. These changes and the loss of freedom for women echo what happened in each of the countries that has been discussed.

TYPES OF MARRIAGE

In pre-Islamic Arabia, there were four kinds of marriage prevalent among the nomads of the peninsula.

1. Marriage by Capture: Woman was considered an asset, the mother of a future swordsman, the cook, the master of the dwelling, and the companion of the man. Women were considered so valuable that tribes attacked their enemies to capture as many as they could.[16] This slavery, arising from the capture of women, is evident in the early days of Islam. Muhammad himself frequently pursued and conquered other tribes' wives and children, whom he distributed as booty among his own followers, as was fully described in the first chapter.

There were four main reasons for capturing women. First, the captive women were held as hostages and only released after ransom money was paid. In this way the victorious tribe was able to strengthen its financial standing or, at least, avert the dangers of destitution and famine. Sometimes the women were sold to other tribes for profit, as Muhammad did when he destroyed the Jewish tribe of Banu Qurayza. Second, it was often cheaper to acquire a woman by fighting than to purchase her in the customary marriage contract. At least two of Muhammad's wives were procured in this way (Safiyya and Juwayriyya), as explained earlier. Third, the hostile tribes wanted to have more women in order to produce more fighting men. Many of the Islamic swordsmen in the third generation after Muhammad were the offspring of women captured in different raids by the founder of Islam and his close associates and successors. Fourth, the tribes who experienced a shortage in their female population found it easier, and probably more economical, to capture others' wives and daughters.[17] This practice is vividly seen in the early days of Muhammad's flight to Medina, when the number of his male followers was many times that of the females. To procure women for his followers, he used the same method as his primitive ancestors, violent forays.

2. *Marriage by Friendship.* In this kind of marriage, the male approached the woman and offered her his friendship. The Arabic word for this sort of marriage was *sadiqa,* which means "girlfriend." The would-be husband approached the woman with the word *"khitb,"* which means, "I am a suitor," and to accept him the lady uttered the word *"nikah,"* which is interpreted as "I wed." There were no witnesses and no wedding ceremony in this type of marriage. The man gave a gift to the bride, a sort of price or gift reflecting the woman's value. This nuptial present was called *"sadaq."*[18]

The children of this type of marriage remained with the mother and the woman's tribe protected her as much after her marriage as before it.[19] The woman could dismiss her husband by merely showing him the door of her tent. In some cases, the woman would offer some nuptial gift, in cash or kind, to have the man of her choice. It is reported that once a rich woman offered herself to Abdullah (Muhammad's father) and said, "If you will take me you can have as many camels as were sacrificed in your stead" (i.e., 100 camels).[20]

3. *Marriage by Contract.* In this kind of marriage, the intended husband drew up a contract with the girl's parents to buy his future wife from them. The purchase price (*mahr*) was paid by the suitor, and the parents, after accepting the offer, delivered their daughter to the bidder. As the selling of the daughter would procure additional income, the father was congratulated on the occasion of the birth of a female child.[21]

The marriage was based on an equal match. One of
the conditions of this sort of marriage was that the children born in the union were to be returned to the girl's
tribe. This condition was always challenged by the husband, who would argue that because he had paid for his
wife the children belonged to him, and eventually a law
(*al-walad li l-frash*) was introduced by which the child was
reckoned to the bed on which he was born. (Muhammad
adopted the same primitive law and added that to
Allah's commandments.) For example, if a captive
woman was pregnant when taken, the child she bore was
considered that of the captor or his tribe.[22] The outcome
of such a law was that the husband could without shame
send his wife to sleep with another man and get pregnant, so that she might bear him a "goodly seed."[23]

4. *Temporary Marriage.* By this arrangement a man
paid a woman for a specified length of time for cohabitation. This type of marriage, *mut'a* ("enjoying a
thing"),[24] continued well into Muhammad's time and
was eventually abolished by 'Umar, the second caliph.
Mut'a was similar to *sadiqa,* or friendship marriage, in
that the woman stayed with her own family and any
children belonged to her tribe. The wife could easily dispose of her temporary husband.

Temporary marriage was basically devised for those
men who were away from their homes on business trips
or military expeditions. They wanted to enjoy the companionship of a young woman for the period that they
would be in her neighborhood and away from their legal
wives. Thus, they would hire a woman for a certain period of time for a specific amount of money for mutual
living and sexual pleasure. It is generally believed that

temporary marriage is the heritage of ancient Arabia and was a sort of national custom, especially among the nomads of the Arabian Peninsula. "It was considered permissible for men and women to form unlicensed unions (trial marriages) terminable at the will of either party."[25]

This early Arab custom, which in reality amounts to harlotry, survived in Islam.[26] It is true that all of the Islamic schools believe it unlawful,[27] but, as will be shown later, the Shiites continue the practice of *mut'a*. According to Falari, the renowned exegete, Muhammad engaged in temporary marriage himself. Based on this view, the Prophet of Allah enjoyed this form of marriage after he started his new religion, possibly as late as his flight to Medina.

Another Muslim historian affirms that in the early days of Islam the Muslim soldier, when he left his town, might enter a temporary marriage and secure a wife for the period of his stay in the assigned place.[28] Al-Bukhari has quoted Abdullah as saying, "We used to participate in the holy battle, led by Allah's apostle, and we had nothing (no wives) with us. So, we said, 'Shall we get ourselves castrated?' He forbade us that and then allowed us to marry women with a temporary contract."[29]

This, however, contradicts the view of the Muslim doctors who maintain that temporary marriage is unlawful in Islam. Muhammad permitted it himself, and by reciting from the Koran—"O you who believe! Make not unlawful the good things which Allah has made lawful for you but commit no transgressing" (5: 87)—he actually made it divine law. The Orthodox Islamic schools, to counter both the Koranic verse and criticism from the protagonists of *mut'a*, created another story that clearly specifies the unlawfulness of temporary marriage. They claim, "The prophet permitted *mut'a*. . . for three days in the year of Awtal, after which he forbade it."[30]

Another group of Muslim teachers maintains that the Prophet permitted *mut'a* for three nights and then he made it unlawful. It is reported that 'Umar, the second caliph and Muhammad's father-in-law, proclaimed that it was definitely unlawful to marry a woman for a temporary period of time. Since that time, the Sunni school does not practice *mut'a*. It is clear from the different traditions that *mut'a* was permitted by Muhammad and he sanctioned it in the Koran. Later, perhaps after the Muslims invaded Egypt, Persia, and Syria, as they confronted the monotheistic religions of Judaism, Christianity, and Zoroastrianism, they then forbade it. Even Ibn 'Abbas, Muhammad's cousin and one of the verse exegetes, is reported to have advocated temporary marriage and only dismissed his views and considered it unlawful just before his death.[31]

Temporary marriage was as lawful as the regular wedding during the first century of Islam.[32] According to al-Tabari, many commentators on the Koran, as late as the second century after the Hegira, maintained that the fixed-period marriage against a specified sum of money was lawful. Al-Suddi, for instance, who died about 129 after the Hegira, held that *mut'a* was a marriage that could be contracted with the permission of the guardian of the girl in the presence of two witnesses. According to him, the two parties should separate after the expiration of the contract term and neither had a claim on the other, nor could they inherit from one another.[33]

During the two hundred years after Muhammad's death Muslim doctors gradually forbade *mut'a*. The

Sunnis, however, devised a new trick to make temporary marriages lawful. They held that if the period of the marriage is not mentioned in the contract, but the man has the intention to dissolve the marriage after a certain period of time, then *mut'a* is valid.

The Shiite school, apparently, has remained faithful to the deeds of the Prophet and consider the *mut'a* an irrevocable contract just like regular marriage with the exception that the period of legal obligation must be stipulated in the contract. No witness is necessary, and no notary public or other official need be present. No clergy is needed to conclude the contract or to supervise the ceremony. For the contract to be valid, the words, "I enjoy you," must be definitely mentioned and the man must pay the wage or "hiring price" in advance.

Upon the expiration of the period, the temporary marriage is ended automatically, and if the couple want to continue being with each other, a new contract with a new bed-wage must be drawn up for the new period of time. There is no divorce in such a marriage, which is based on sexual relations alone, and repudiation is impossible. In fact, the man is not even obliged to provide food or shelter for the woman. At the expiration date, the woman has to wait forty-five days before she enters into another in-bed agreement with someone else. But since there is usually no witness to the marriage and separation, the woman could enter into another contract immediately after the previous contract had expired.

As was mentioned, the temporary marriage is practiced today only by Shiite Muslims. These people are the followers of Muhammad's cousin and son-in-law, 'Ali, who is reported to have said: "Verily, the prophet prohibited the *mut'a* marriage of woman on the day (of the conquest) of Khaybar [see chapter 1] and he prohibited the eating of the domestic ass."[34] If this quotation is valid, then 'Ali opposed temporary marriage, but his followers don't seem to agree with him.

The Shiite clergy hold that temporary marriage is definitely sanctioned by Allah in the Koran: "but those of whom you seek enjoyment (*istamt'atum*) give unto them their pay (reward) as a duty and there is no sin for you by mutual agreement after such lawful due." (Koran 4: 24) According to this school, the words "wage" or "reward" in the above verse is the proof of its permissibility.

We do not intend to enter here into the discussion, or the dispute, between the opponents and proponents of temporary marriage. Rather, we shall continue by explaining permanent marriage, or the union by contract, that is accepted by all the Islamic schools and is considered by the Muslim as one of the most progressive laws in the world.

THE CONDITIONS FOR MARRIAGE

Contract

Islamic law necessitates a contract for each and every marriage without which the union is not valid. This requirement is not without precedent. The Babylonian code, for instance, had stipulated long before Muhammad that if the marriage contract is not drawn up the marriage is not legal. The Code of Hammurabi, which was promulgated during his empire (Hammurabi died in about 1750 B.C.E.), states: "If a man takes a wife, but did not draw up her contract, that woman is no wife."[35] This law, too, is rooted among the customs of the ancient people living in that part of the world. The Law of Eshnunna, for example, which is almost two hundred years older than the Code of Hammurabi and dates back as far as 2000 B.C.E., states: "If a man marries another man's daughter without approval of her parents, even if she lives one year with him, she is not his wife."[36]

The Sumerian laws, such as the Law of Ur-Nammu and the Law of Lipit-Ishtar, which go back twenty-two centuries before our era, stipulate the requirement of the marriage contract very clearly. Thus, Muhammad's law regarding the marriage contract is not unprecedented. There are two features in the Law of Eshnunna that should be noted, however.

1. The Law of Eshnunna stipulated the approval of the girl's parents in order for the marriage to be legal; in this the ancient Semitic law is superior to that of Muhammad, because the latter required only the approval of the father or a male guardian and not the approval of both parents. In other words, Islamic law is more patriarchal and male oriented.

2. According to the Law of Eshnunna, in the absence of the marriage contract the union is not legally recognized, but the man and woman could live together if they pleased. In Islam, a woman who lives with a man without a marriage contract is committing fornication and is liable to receive a penalty of not less than one hundred lashes if discovered.

Religion

A Muslim girl may not marry any man she chooses because the basic condition for marriage is that her husband must be a Muslim. "And do not give (a Muslim woman) in marriage to idolators until they have accepted Islam, and certainly a believing slave is better than an idolater even though he should please you." (Koran 2: 221)

The word "idolater" in the above verse is defined to mean a nonbeliever—whether a Jew, Christian, Buddhist, or Zoroastrian—anyone but a Muslim. Thus, according to the Koran, no Muslim girl may marry a man whose religion differs from hers.

Does the same law apply to men as well? Not exactly, since a Muslim man can marry any woman who is not an atheist. In other words, a man may have a Christian, a Jewish, or even a Zoroastrian woman as his wife, because Muhammad's scripture explicitly allows such a marriage: "And the chaste from among the believing women and the chaste from among those who have been given the book before you (are lawful for you) when you have given them their marriage portion taking them in marriage." (Koran 5: 5) The phrase "those who have been given the book before you" refers to Jews and Christians, who have their own Bibles.

In comparing the status of men and women in the Koran, we find out that the two are not treated equally. Although a man is allowed to marry a non-Muslim woman, the woman is totally prohibited from marrying any non-Muslim man.

Muslims believe that the new order proposed by Muhammad as a religion is based on justice and equality. They maintain that no other religion has ever treated women more fairly than Islam, and yet we see that in the very first condition laid out for marriage the male gets the better share. The divine law is made in the man's favor; the woman is disadvantaged.

Is Allah biased against women? Does Allah, the Supreme Being, like an ordinary pre-Islamic man, favor the man over the women? Or, is it Muhammad, the lawgiver, who wants to ensure the supremacy of the male under the name of a new religion? It is surely the Prophet, and not Allah, who debases the woman and deprives her from the right to choose her mate.

The Legal Age for Marriage

There is no specific age for marriage stated in the Koran, but the tradition of Muhammad and his close associates reveals that a man, no matter how old he is, may contract and consummate a marriage with a girl as young as nine years old. In fact, Muhammad himself married Aisha, the daughter of Abu Bakr, when she was six years of age, and took her to his bed three years later. (The consummation of this marriage is fully described in chapter 1.) Thus, child-marriage, which was a remnant of primitive Arab rites (pagan Semitic tribes used to draw up contracts in which the guardians chose mates for their underage children), was perpetuated by Muhammad and made a divine law. "It is usual," writes Jones, "for orthodox Muslims to claim that a child-marriage, though not enjoined either in the Koran or traditions, is part of the very fabric of Islam. They contend that the custom is sanctioned by the practice of Muhammad, who himself married a child-wife and gave in marriage a child-wife."[37]

Today, in the civilized world, the cohabitation of a fully grown man with a female child of nine or ten would be considered child molestation, not marriage, and the offender would be prosecuted under the law. Nonetheless, some Islamic jurists try to justify Muhammad's action in marrying Aisha when she was still a child. One Muslim doctor had this to say: "Aisha's Nikah [marriage] was performed in Mecca long before the details of the Islamic laws were revealed to the holy prophet, and therefore, her marriage at nine can be no agreement [justification] for the marriage of a minor."[38] This poor excuse is not only contrary to the fact, but also falls short of justification for Muhammad's behavior because:

1. According to all reliable Islamic history books, only three years passed from the day Muhammad married Aisha to the day he took her to his bed. During this period, no law regarding the marriage age of the girl was enjoined. In fact, during the entire life of Muhammad no specific rule was set down determining the minimum age of a girl for marriage.

2. If the details of Islamic law were revealed to the Prophet after his marriage to Aisha, then he should have amended his marriage in a lawful manner to evade any criticism. On the contrary, Muhammad seemed to have enjoyed his union with his child-wife, as he spent most of his harem time with her and she was his favorite.

3. From the beginning of Islam to the present time, a great many Muslim males have followed Muhammad's example and married minors. For instance, 'Umar, who

was one of Muhammad's closest friends, his immediate successor, and is believed to have been very orthodox in trying to carry out the Koranic law to the letter, married 'Ali's daughter, Umm Kulthum (Muhammad's granddaughter) when she was barely ten years old. 'Umar was then in his late fifties.

Islamic chronology is full of such examples of child-marriage. This demonstrates that taking a minor as a wife did not end with Muhammad's death—on the contrary, it became a law. Almost all of the caliphs of the Umayyad, 'Abbasid, and Fatimid dynasties practiced child-marriage.

4. The very author who tries to justify Muhammad's marriage to a child-wife contradicts himself a few lines later, when he says: "Fiqh [Islamic jurisprudence], however, recognizes the legality of the minor marriage when contracted by a lawful guardian."[39]

If the legality of child-marriage is accepted by Islamic jurisprudence, the apologists cannot justify Muhammad's marriage to a nine-year-old by saying it was performed "long before the details of Islamic law were revealed to the holy prophet." The phrase "details of Islamic law" is synonymous with jurisprudence, and jurisprudence recognizes such marriages. In other words, this attempt at justification nullifies itself because it simultaneously condemns and redeems Muhammad's action.

According to Islamic law, the guardian of the girl (her father or grandfather)* could negotiate the terms of

---

*In Islamic jurisprudence, "guardian" usually means the paternal close kin, such as father, grandfather, or uncle. No woman has the right to appoint herself as a guardian of her own daughter as long as her father- or brother-in-law is living.

marriage with either the suitor or his parents, just as Abu Bakr (Aisha's father) discussed his daughter's terms of marriage with Muhammad when Aisha was but six years old. 'Ali did the same with 'Umar, when 'Ali's daughter, Umm Kulthum, was a mere child.

Marriage is a contract and is simply based on the mutual consent and agreement, oral or written, of the two parties involved. Marriage, therefore, is a secular contract and not a religious rite. If the bride or suitor is a minor, his or her guardian can enter into the terms of marriage even without the child's consent.

Those concluding a marriage contract must be sane and have reached the age of legal majority. "Among the Shafais [school], a woman cannot personally consent to marriage. The presence of the guardian (*wali*) is essentially necessary to give validity to the contract. The guardian's intervention is required by the Shafais and Malikis to supplement the presumed incapacity of the woman to understand the nature of the contract."[40] Thus, in Muhammad's law, the woman has no capacity to conclude her own marriage, even if she were of the legal age to do so.

Some Islamic schools of thought, however, such as the Hanafi and Shiite, may allow a woman to decide her own marriage. In contrast, other schools do not believe that a woman *ever* has a right to conclude her own marriage. In such Muslim communities, if an adult woman marries the man of her choice without the approval of her guardian, that marriage is completely invalid. Aisha is reported to have said: "Every woman who marries without consent of her guardian, her marriage is null and void," and she repeated herself three times to emphasize the statement.[41]

It is noteworthy that Aisha, who outlived Muhammad by many years, is considered to be one of the best sources of her husband's words and deeds, and some two hundred narrations from Muhammad believed by all schools to be authentic are attributed to her. Her narrations are taken seriously by some schools because it is argued that she is merely reflecting her husband's ideas.

It is indisputable that child-marriage was practiced during Muhammad's time. He perpetuated it, and ever since his death this sort of marriage has tantalized a great number of Muslim clergies, jurists, and theologians.

One such example is Imam Ja'far as-Sadiq, one of the main sources of the Shiite school and the great-grandson of Muhammad. Ja'far as-Sadiq is considered to be one of the foremost scholars in the field of Shiite jurisprudence. This man, the direct descendent of the apostle of Allah, is reported to have said: "Virtuous is the one whose daughter does not start menses at her father's house."[42] By this he means that a girl must be given away in marriage before she begins her menstrual cycles or monthly periods, and any father who does so is a true Muslim and virtuous believer.

In some schools, the ward, "on attaining puberty," may repudiate the marriage contracted by her guardian. The marriage, however, is perfectly valid up to that time. Sometimes infants may be contracted in marriage by their guardians. Thus, the marriage of an infant or an underage boy or girl is lawful if it is contracted by the nearest male kindred. What happens when such infants attain majority? Could they themselves sanction the marriages that had been contracted in their infancies? Apparently the male can give his consent without approval of a guardian, but there is a difference of opinion with regard to the woman on whether she can give her consent without the approval of her guardian.

THE BRIDE-PRICE IN MARRIAGE

According to the Koran, any Muslim male who wishes to get married must stipulate a certain amount of money in his marriage contract as a bride-price. The specific sum should be paid to his future wife or her immediate male kinfolk (i.e., her father or grandfather). One of the Muslim authorities in jurisprudence said: "A dowry (*mahr*) must also be settled on the woman according to the holy Koran."[43]

This word, *mahr*, which is used by all Muslim jurists as well as the layman in the street, is not, curiously enough, mentioned in the Koran at all, not even once! Jones said, "It is a curious fact, however, that the term, *mahr*, is nowhere used in the Koran, though it is common in the tradition."[44] There are, however, other terminologies used instead of *mahr*, which are derived from the pre-Islamic period when the Arabs worshiped different deities. The word *mahr* is apparently the Arabic pronunciation of the old Hebrew word *mohr*. Instead, the word *ajr* is used, which actually means wage or reward. For instance, if you hire someone to work for you, at the end of the day or week you pay his wages (*ajr*). The plural of *ajr* is *ujur*, meaning the wages for the hired one.

Some commentators on the Koran have translated the term *ajr* to mean reward or gift given to the bride.[45]

The other terminology used in the Koran for dowry is *fariza,* meaning what is obligatory for the man to pay to his wife before or after the marriage, for having her in wedlock. *Ajr,* as used in the Koran, may be translated to mean the hired-wage, bride-price, bed-wage, or reward for cohabitation.

The Friendship Gift (Sadaq)

The Koran states: "And give unto the women (whom ye marry) free gift of their marriage portions." (Koran 4: 4) The "free gift" is the translation of *sadaq,* which, as was explained earlier, is the gift or money exchanged in the friendship-type of marriage. In pre-Islamic days, a friendly union of a man and woman necessitated the payment of money or other kind of property, which the suitor would usually hand over to his prospective wife. She could regain her freedom by returning the *sadaq* to her man. *Sadaq,* according to some authors, was a gift besides a bride-price. The bride-price was usually paid to the girl's parents, whereas, the friendship gift (*sadaq*) was given exclusively to the wife herself. Under Muhammad, this custom was changed and now only *mahr* (dowry) is paid either to the father of the girl or to her nearest male kin.

The Bride-Price for Slave Girls

In Islamic communities, men have traditionally been permitted to take as mates two classes of women: free women and concubines (captured women or slave girls).

If a slave girl was to be married to a free man, i.e., her master, she was then freed and given a bride-price, unless her master agreed to give her freedom as the bride-price. Muhammad himself kept some captive girls as concubines, and instead of a bride-price, he freed them and added them to his harem.

On the other hand, if a slave girl was married to another slave, a wage or reward had to be stipulated in the marriage contract. It should be noted that although slavery was abolished in most countries quite a long time ago, it is not prohibited in Islam, and prominent Muslim jurists have thus far not denounced this institution. Muslims believe that the Koran is the indisputable word of Allah; therefore, no true Muslim faithful would ever dare to defy the text of this holy book. Thus, slavery is an accepted precept in Muhammad's law. The Koran also states that if a Muslim army conquers a town of nonbelievers or defeats enemy soldiers, they may make the vanquished people their slaves and sell or dispose of them any way they please. Because the institution of slavery is fully recognized by the Koran, many of the laws regarding the taking and handling of slaves are being taught in Muslim religious schools and universities even in modern times.

The wages due for cohabitation with a slave girl are specified in the Koran: "So marry them [slave girls] with the permission of their masters and give them their bed wages justly." (Koran 4: 25) Thus, a bride-price must be paid for slaves as well as free women.

In accordance with the text of the Koran and the tradition of Muhammad, the two main sources of Islamic laws, the payment of the bride-price must be made at the time of marriage, whether the bride is a free woman or a slave. If the bride-price is not explicitly specified in the marriage contract, it has to be determined and paid later on. If for some reason or other, the payments were not made soon after the marriage and the husband died, this deferred payment would be charged against his property and deducted from what he left as his legacy to be paid to his widow.

The Amount of the Bride-Price

The minimum amount of the bride-price is not mentioned in the Koran or in later Islamic jurisprudence, just as the minimum age for marriage is not clearly specified; it all depends on the husband's wealth and the position of the woman. This is clearly stipulated in the Muslim scripture: "the wealthy according to his means, and the poor according to his means." (Koran 2: 236) Thus, Islam considers the woman as a commodity, and her price is determined by her position. If she is rich, from an affluent family with higher standing, or beautiful and well-bred, her bride-price would be higher. On the other hand, if the prospective bride belongs to a lower stratum of the community and is from a poor family without influential background, her price would be much lower, no matter how rich her suitor may be.

A woman is bought according to her position and her bride-price is paid on that basis. The marriage price for Muhammad's daughter, Fatima, who was given to 'Ali, when Muhammad did not have much money and 'Ali was equally poor, amounted to only 400 dirhams (some writers argue that it was equivalent to the price of 'Ali's armor). The bride-price for Muhammad's granddaughter, Umm Kulthum, however, when she was handed over as a wife to 'Umar, the second caliph, is recorded by most Muslim historians to be 10,000 gold dinars, because at that time 'Ali, the bride's father, was a rich man, thanks to his share of the booty received from plundering other communities. He possessed many orchards, cultivated lands, date-palm trees, houses, horses, camels, sheep, goats, cash money, and many male and female slaves. Thus, Umm Kulthum's status was much higher than that of her mother.

The Ancient Origin of the Bride-Price (Mahr and Ajr)

It was mentioned previously that the Arabic word *mahr* (dowry) is derived from a Hebrew word, *mohr*. Zimmerman maintains that the two may have originated from the ancient Assyrian word *mahiru*, meaning "price."[46] This suggests that the man actually buys his wife from her father. Koschner supports this theory by arguing that marriage in ancient Babylonia was merely the purchasing of the woman, and the price the husband would pay for his wife was called *mahiru*. The girl's father would receive money or its equivalent from the bridegroom or his father.[47]

Koschner goes on to define *tirhatum*, a word from Middle Assyrian law (ca. 1400 B.C.E), as "bride-price." Kohler, another linguist, translated it as "woman-price" (*frauen-preis*).[48]

Tirhatum, in Assyrian, is derived from the word

which means sexual intercourse. The *mahr*, therefore, is the price paid by a man to cohabit with a woman. As was noted previously, the word *ajr* used in the Koran is the price of acquiring a woman in wedlock, the price of a woman practically hired to live with her husband as long as he wants her around. So we observe that the Koran, by using the word *ajr*, is directly taking after the Assyrian law prevalent in Northern Arabia and Assyria in pre-Islamic days. Consequently, Muhammad requires his faithful followers to pay a price to a woman for her sexual services.

The bride-price is much more ancient than even the Assyrian law, let alone Islamic jurisprudence. The Code of Hammurabi (the set of laws promulgated by the ancient king of Babylonia) in many sections refers to the bride-price. The following is quoted to demonstrate how the ancient Babylonians legalized the bride-price: "If a man, who had the betrothal gift brought to the house of his father-in-law and paid the marriage price, has then looked upon another woman, and says to his prospective father-in-law, 'I shall not marry your daughter,' the father of the daughter shall keep whatever was brought to him."[49] One can easily infer from this law why the different schools in Islam require that the bride's guardian should draw up the marriage contract for his daughter, as he is usually the one who received the *ajr* for consenting to the wedding.

Another law stipulates, "If a man has had the betrothal gift brought to the house of his prospective father-in-law and paid the marriage-price, and the father of the girl then says, 'I shall not give you my daughter,' he shall pay back double whatever had been brought to him."[50]

There are more laws concerning the marriage price in Hammurabi's Code, but two examples suffice to show the ancient origin of *ajr* (bride-price) in Islamic jurisprudence.

Bride-Price: Divine Revelation?

Muhammad himself paid the bride-price to his first wife, Khadija, almost fifteen years before he declared himself to be the Prophet of Allah and began revealing the verses of the Koran. Hence, the bride-price could not have been a divinely inspired tenet of Muhammad's new faith, as orthodox Muslims insist, because this custom, like so many of the Koranic laws, had been in practice some two thousand years prior to Muhammad and his revelations. Most of the marriage laws that appear in the Koran were originated by the tyrant-despots of the ancient world.

The question, therefore, that believers in the Koran's inerrant truth must answer is why Allah's revealed laws are so similar to the laws of ancient pagan monarchs. Why would Allah—who is explicitly described in the Koran as the "Knower," the "Sovereign Lord," the "Majestic," the "Superb," and the "Compeller" (Koran 59: 22–23)—enjoin all his faithful to marry according to non-believers' rules?

Could not Allah—the Creator, the Shaper-out-of-naught, and the Fashioner (Koran 59: 24)—have devised marriage laws that did not debase women and reduce their position to that of a mere commodity, which could be sold and handed over after "its" price was paid? Couldn't Allah have made a more equitable law?

In comparing Hammurabi's law to the Koranic tenets with respect to the bride-price, we find that Muhammad's law is in no way an improvement over that of the king of Babylonia, and in modern Islam marriage is still the act of purchasing a wife, just as it was two thousand years before the time of Muhammad.

According to the tenets of Islam, if no bride-price is mentioned in the contract, the wife is entitled to an appropriate payment. The real meaning of bride-price as a form of hiring or payment for services is well understood when we consider the fact that a woman may refuse to let her husband enjoy sexual intercourse until she receives the bride-price. She has the right to do so. As long as she is not paid the specified price, she may stay away from her husband's bed. As soon as he pays, however, he obtains full authority over his wife.

If a woman dies after the marriage is consummated, her right to a bride-price is not transferred to her family. But if her husband dies at the same time, the wife's heirs can take the dower (*mahr*) out of the husband's estate. If a minor girl who had been given away in marriage by her guardian dies before she reaches legal maturity, her husband inherits her dowry, not her parents.

If consummation does not occur after the girl is married, she receives one half of her bride-price. Also, it is customary for the parents to give to the bride a trousseau. In such cases, if she is divorced, she must receive back whatever was originally given to her by her parents, plus the bride-price. These laws further demonstrate that marriage in Islam is merely a sales transaction.

CONCLUSION

Muslim theologians and clerics maintain that the position of woman has improved under Islam, and Muhammad is hailed by them as the greatest emancipator of women from the cruelty and oppression of the Dark Ages of Arabia, the pre-Islamic days.

This, however, is not true. As was discussed earlier in the chapter, pre-Islamic women enjoyed much more freedom than Muslim females do. They could choose their own mates, were free to move around at will, conducted their own business affairs, and shared the same privileges as their male counterparts. Lyall notes:

> The place of women in the society of pagan Arabia was appreciably higher than that which they hold under Al-Islam. They had much liberty which was afterwards denied them. . . . They were much freer in their movements than they became after the ordinance of the veil had been prescribed. . . . In many cases, they selected their mates for themselves, instead of having to accept the choice for them by their guardians.[51]

Nicholson agrees: "On the whole, their position was high and their influence great. . . . They were regarded not as slaves and chattels, but as equals and companions."[52]

Islam, on the other hand, treats women as inferior beings and women have lost their independence through the advent of this religion. For example, the lot of Indian women changed when Islam was forcefully imposed upon them. The inferior position of women in Pakistan and part of India today is undoubtedly the result of the influx of Muhammad's religion in the subcontinent, which started as early as eleventh century of our era.

It is clear, then, that pre-Islamic women enjoyed some sort of independence and liberty before they were forced to accept the religion of the Muslim war-wagers, who would stop at nothing short of surrender and submission. Literally, *Islam* means "submission" to the will of Allah, but this religion came with force, changed the ideology of the ancient world by force, and reduced women to the status of slaves and chattel through an iron fist and the sword.

Widespread movements composed of educated and liberal-minded Muslim writers have become prevalent, calling for reform with regard to the status of women. For example, in Turkey and Tunisia, new regulations were passed which instituted a number of legal reforms especially affecting women. A minimum legal age for marriage was established. It stipulated that the marriages that were contracted and licensed by Muslim clerics were only valid if registered with the government agencies.

Reform in women's education has also occurred. In 1893, for instance, Turkish women were permitted to attend classes in the medical colleges of Istanbul University for the first time. Six years later, women were allowed to take part in regular medical studies. Courses for women in other sectors of the university began as early as February 1914. This was a dramatic change in a country that was the official seat of the Muslim caliphate for four hundred years.

Iraq (the modern name of ancient Babylonia), which

was under the rule of the Ottoman Empire for centuries, enjoyed almost the same liberty given to Turkish women in Istanbul. In 1899, the first regular girls' school was opened, which began the coeducation system in Baghdad University.

Regular classes for girls in primary school began in 1917 in Iran. Tehran University, a latecomer to Middle Eastern higher education, accepted women as full-time students shortly after World War II. In the meantime, as of 1935, women were allowed to get jobs in different government offices, something that even a decade earlier had been unthinkable.

The age of marriage for both Iranian girls and boys was raised, and all of the marriage contracts had to be registered. Child-marriage was prohibited by the law, and severe punishment was prescribed for those who concluded any wedding contract for minors.

In Tunisia, the minimum age for marriage was also raised—eighteen years for boys and sixteen for girls. This was raised once more a little later to twenty and eighteen, respectively.

In Turkey, Tunisia, and Iran, the right of the guardians who could enter into a marriage contract on behalf of minors was rescinded and anyone who committed such a felony was liable to prosecution. All of these reforms were possible in places in which a strong centralized government defied the Islamic laws of marriage and curbed the authority of the Muslim fundamentalist clergies in the *Shariat* (religious procedure). Islamic jurisprudence came under severe criticism by liberal-minded intellectuals who believed child-marriage to be inhuman.

Despite these changes, Muslim jurisprudence concerning marriage is still incomplete and sometimes inefficient. Although Muhammad claimed the laws to be those ordered by Allah, in reality they are based on nomadic rites and traditions, and the inequality of the sexes prevalent in them merely reflects the ancient culture with which Muhammad was familiar.

3

POLYGAMY, CONCUBINAGE, AND SLAVERY

Marry of the women, who seem good to you, two, three or four.

—Koran 4: 3

Although the above-quoted verse of the Koran permits each Muslim male to marry legally up to four wives concurrently, Muhammad, as we have seen, filled his harem with at least a dozen young wives. Ironically, he was monogamous for most of his life and it wasn't until he was fifty-three or fifty-four that he started to expand his harem. According to some Islamic historians, he married a total of nineteen times, consummating the union with fourteen wives, all of whom were in his harem concurrently.

As shown in chapter 1, a verse in the Koran gave him special privileges, allowing him to practice this double standard (Koran 33: 50). He was permitted to take as wives all of his cousins from his mother's and father's side, those who fled with him from Mecca, and those who joined him later in Medina. For all practical purposes the law placed no limits on his caprice.

In addition, he was given permission to cohabit with as many slave girls as he could acquire. These were the captured women, the "booty" of his numerous forays. The female slaves that came into his possession in those raids became, in accordance with Koranic law, his chattel, regardless of whether they had been single or married at the time of captivity. Islam did not recognize the marital status of any wife whose husband, in defending his country or tribe, fell in battle fighting off Muslim invaders. This held true for all Muslim men who acquired chattel through raids. They could have as many female slaves as they could afford.

Another noteworthy feature of verse 33: 50 is that it exempted Muhammad from paying the usual bride-price to any woman who was willing to join his harem. Recall from the last chapter that in order to marry a woman the prospective husband had first to pay a certain amount of money as the bride-price and that no marriage contract was valid unless the bride-price was clearly specified in it. With the revelation of verse 33: 50, Allah made lawful the union of any woman who gave herself as a gift to his Prophet—with the condition, of course, that: "the Prophet desire to marry her." The exceptional nature of this privilege for the Prophet is understood at the end of the verse as follows: "[This is] a special privilege for thee above the rest of the believers."

For the ordinary Muslim man, the Koran (4: 3) decrees: "Marry of the women, who seem good to you, two or three or four." Thus, the institution of polygamy was divinely legalized by Muhammad in his scripture and on the basis of such permission, many millions of Muslim males have had more than one wife in wedlock.

Some apologists, however, try to justify this humiliating institution by saying that Islam, though it permits polygamy, does not enjoin it: "The passage permits polygamy under certain circumstances; it does not enjoin it nor even permit it unconditionally."[1] This is certainly a poor defense against the criticism of those who believe that polygamy is a remnant of savagery and is detrimental to the socioeconomic life of any community in which it is permitted. Even some Muslim women who are directly affected by the Koranic law regarding polygamy close their eyes and pretend that the commandment of Allah in Muhammad's scripture is merely a misunderstanding:

> Very few people seem to realize that the Koran lays down rather stringent conditions about taking the second wife while the first is alive . . . but, no matter what the conditions are, no man can marry more than once unless he can treat all of his wives with justice and equality.[2]

This writer does not seem to realize that polygamy has been in practice in Islam ever since Muhammad permitted it in the Koran. The law permitting a Muslim male to marry as many as four wives concurrently is most certainly a discriminatory decree against women and to the benefit of men in every Muslim society. This one-sided privilege, given solely to men, leads over time to the segregation of women from men, and women are gradually driven out of most socioeconomic activities, as is largely the case in the Muslim world today. The results of polygamy are conspiracies, quarrels, and jealousies among the different wives, and sometimes beating, death threats, even poisoning and infanticide. Moreover, women under these conditions are humiliated and are looked upon as slave girls, or even as a commodity. Add to all of these the hatred among the children of different mothers and the inferiority complexes resulting from the tragedy of such a family life and there is little to recommend this lifestyle.

Nonetheless, there are quite a number of Muslim theologians who maintain very optimistically that since the condition for marrying more than one wife is treating them equally and with justice, few male Muslims dare to be polygamists, except those who can afford a separate quarter as well as living expenses for each wife. But this is hardly the case. In fact, many Muslims have been polygamists, especially in the first five centuries of Islamic history when so many Muslims became wealthy due to forays and the spoils of war.

Some Westerners and non-Muslim writers seem to be quite unfamiliar with the actual social history of Islam, or they are completely misled by the Muslim apologists. Here is an example:

> This divine command virtually amounts to prohibition of polygamy, the taking of multiple wives, because it is extremely difficult, if not impossible, for a man to treat several wives equally. The polygamy is to be practiced only in unusual extenuating circumstances.[3]

Nothing could be further from the truth. Since the advent of Islam, many Muslims have been polygamists and, as the above writer notes, practically none of them have been able to treat their wives with equality and justice. The best example is Muhammad himself. He originated the law of polygamy and he advised equality among the different wives, but he could never practice what he preached! Muslim biographers tell us that he preferred Aisha, his teenaged wife, to the others. He stayed in her home more, and this little, slim child-wife meant more to him than the rest of his wives put together. When he was criticized, he sheepishly admitted: "God, this is as far as I can go in controlling my inclinations. But, I have no power over what you own and I don't [meaning love]."[4]

As described in chapter 1, his aging wife Sauda offered to give up her cohabitation turn in favor of Aisha in order to remain a member of his harem. As a result of this arrangement, Muhammad agreed not to divorce her. "Aisha was the one he loved the most and all of his other wives knew it."[5]

Next to Aisha, Muhammad showed preferences for Zaynab, Hafsa, and his concubine, Mariya. His scandalous love affair with the Coptic concubine led to the jealousy of Hafsa, a sexual boycott by Hafsa and Aisha, and then retaliation by Muhammad, who spent an entire month with Mariya to spite his wives. A "revelation of threats" from Allah finally put an end to the incident. These are hardly examples of equal and just treatments of his wives.

After Muhammad passed away, his successor and father-in-law, Abu Bakr, also had several women in his harem. 'Umar, 'Uthman, and 'Ali—the second, third, and fourth caliphs, respectively—had many wives at one and the same time. Hassan, the fifth caliph and Muhammad's grandson, followed the practice of marrying four wives at the same time, then after a few weeks, divorcing the entire harem and marrying another four women. He was accordingly nicknamed "the excessive marrier." Similarly, all of the caliphs of the Umayyad, 'Abbasid, and Fatimid dynasties were polygamists. Under the Ottoman Empire, which ruled the vast territory of Asia, Europe, and North Africa, from 1495 to the First World War, the harem was a common feature of the wealthy man's domain. Especially among the courtiers and men in higher society, polygamy was practiced endlessly. Hundreds of thousands of young, captive women were used as chattel and changed hands continuously. They came from Greece, Bulgaria, Romania, Yugoslavia, Syria, Mesopotamia, Arabia, Egypt, Cypress—even as far as Austria and southern Russia. Harem life has been the subject of fiction and nonfiction alike, as that style of life held curiosity for many.

Even today, the so-called House of Saud, which rules Saudi Arabia, especially Mecca and Medina, and is considered to be one of the most orthodox Muslim communities in the world, enjoys the practice of polygamy. Almost all of the rich men from the king down to the minor prince *(amir)* in one form or another can be described as polygamists.

Did all of these polygamist Muslims treat their wives with equality and justice in the past? Are all men with more than one wife today in such countries as Pakistan, India, Sudan, Egypt, Syria, and Iraq, just and impartial to their wives?

We agree wholeheartedly with those apologists who contend that treating several wives equally is "extremely difficult if not impossible." Such difficulties, however, have not proved to be a sufficient obstacle to stop the practice of polygamy in the past or even today. Polygamy is practiced by both rich and poor Muslim males, who in many cases don't have any idea what the word justice means. This group includes peasants, farmers, villagers, merchants of the bazaar, and small craftsmen—most of whom are either illiterate or have meager educations, which is not enough to enable them to differentiate between justice and injustice in the matrimonial behavior. From generation to generation they have heard that Allah has sanctioned the taking of multiple wives and that He will provide for their subsistence. After all, according to the Koran and Muslim belief, it is Allah who gives happiness and prosperity to anyone He chooses and it is also Allah who abases whom He will:

> O Allah! Owner of Sovereignty! Thou givest sovereignty unto whom Thou wilt and Thou withdrawest sovereignty from whom Thou wilt. Thou exalt whom Thou wilt and Thou abasest whom Thou wilt. In Thy hand is the good. Lo! Thou art able to do all things. (Koran 3: 26)

According to this doctrine, everything is in the hands of Allah. He bestows riches on anyone He favors, and makes poor whomever displeases him. If a man marries four wives, it is Allah's will. If the children die from malnutrition and hunger, it is Allah's will. If the husband treats his wife with harshness and even savagery, it is their lot, which has been prepared for them by Allah. If they are killed in war, it is Allah who wanted them dead!

In short, Allah is responsible for both good and evil, and nothing happens that He does not will. That is why one so frequently hears the idiomatic phrase *In sha-Allah* (God willing) in the Muslim world. Whatever a Muslim does is Allah's will! Therefore, the polygamist feels no shame or remorse. Moreover, taking multiple wives is sanctioned by Allah in His scripture, and a true believer has no right to question or doubt the validity of the Koranic tenets. Like the average believers of any traditional religion, the vast majority of Muslims follow the customs of Islam and perform their religious ceremonies without any thought or question about the rationale and history behind them. The Muslim male is merely following the lead of his Prophet, who had a harem full of young wives. Since he is given the right to marry up to four wives in the Koran, he does not care much about any inequality or injustice resulting from this inhuman and barbarous custom.

The wealthy polygamist holds that if he maintains a subsistence level of living for each of his wives, justice is done. For him, the command of "treating them equally" means only that he must provide each one with the same upkeep and have sexual intercourse with each of them in turns.

Despite the obviously repugnant nature of polygamy, Muslim apologists try to find convincing excuses for it. Let us examine some of these rationalizations.

APOLOGISTS' ARGUMENTS FOR POLYGAMY

Polygamy Eliminates Prostitution

Some apologists argue that a man who can afford to marry more than one wife is actually helping a society that has more women than men by preventing women from becoming prostitutes! Polygamy supposedly eliminates the necessity for unattached women to resort to prostitution as a means of survival. There are several arguments that can be made against this contention.

First, although there are some countries in the world today in which the number of women is somewhat higher than the number of men, the women in these countries certainly have means of supporting themselves other than prostitution. Furthermore, the inhabitants of many of these countries are not all Muslims, so polygamy laws do not apply to these women. Second, even if there are a few Muslim communities in which the number of women surpasses that of men, these are the exceptional cases and a universal law should not be instituted for the sake of rare cases. Third, despite the fact that polygamy has been practiced by all Muslim communities since Muhammad sanctioned it through special laws, prostitution has not been eliminated anywhere except in the most conservative places where there are severe punishments against it. As Samuel Zwemer states, "Polygamy has not diminished licentiousness in any Muslim land, but everywhere it increased it."[6]

Public prostitution is a commonplace in Islamic

countries. From Casablanca to Egypt and as far as Indonesia, there are women who put themselves at the disposal of men for money. The nude belly-dancing of Istanbul, Beirut, Cairo, Damascus, and Baghdad is world renowned. Ironically these cities were the seats of the Muslim caliphs at different periods of time. If even in the heart of the Islamic empire at the height of its power this moral aberration was manifested in a most unorthodox way, then it stands to reason that the institution of polygamy has not been a major innovation for stopping prostitution.

Nonetheless, some Muslim apologists believe that only Islam can save modern society from the chronic ill of prostitution. For instance, Maulana Muhammad 'Ali has this to say in defense of polygamy:

> It may be added here that polygamy in Islam is both, in theory and practice, an exception not a rule, and as an exception, it is a remedy for many of the evils of modern civilization. It is not only the preponderance of females over males that necessitates polygamy in certain cases, but there is a variety of other circumstances which require polygamy to be adopted under exceptional circumstances, not only for the moral but also the physical welfare of society. . . . Prostitution which is in the increase with the advancement of civilization, and which is eating into it like a canker, with its constant increase of bastardy, is practically unknown to the countries where polygamy is allowed as a remedial measure.[7]

As we already pointed out, prostitution is prevalent in the countries in which polygamy is allowed. In fact, polygamy and easy divorce, two of the major Islamic tenets given as prerogatives to the male, are among the main causes of prostitution in the Muslim world:

> In spite of official disapproval of Islam, public prostitution has never been abolished, and although public women and their procurers are regarded as law breakers, they are to be found in practically all Muhammadan lands.[8]

Polygamy Originated as a Means of Providing for Widows in Time of War

Some maintain that historically polygamy was the result of the numerous skirmishes of the Muslim warriors in the early days of Islam and the rapid decrease in the male population due to the casualties. The Prophet, therefore, enjoined polygamy so that the small number of surviving men could take care of the many widows left unattended after their husbands lost their lives.[9]

Opposing this theory is the fact that Muhammad's raids upon the other Arabian tribes were only local and limited in number and scope. Hence, there was no need for a universal law of polygamy. The number of Muslim soldiers who fell in these forays was not of the magnitude to necessitate such a sweeping provision.

Moreover, in other cultures polygamy is never considered a reasonable solution for a situation in which there is an increase of women over men. If this were the only criterion for adopting polygamy, then the Russian and German governments, after the loss of some fifty million of their male populations as the result of World War II, should have had a very good reason to imitate the Koranic law and introduce the institution of polygamy. But of course this "remedy"was not adopted in those countries or in Japan or the United States of America.

Polygamy Is the Only Legitimate Means of Satisfying Male Sexual Desires

Some Muslim writers argue that men are created in such a way that they need more than one wife. Monogamy, they argue, is an insufficient outlet for satisfying men's sexual desires. The result of this situation has been prostitution:

> Man, by nature and instinct, is polygamous. . . . Wives, in at least twenty percent of the cases, are [because of their monthly menstrual period] unwilling to give satisfaction to their husbands.[10]

The Muslim apologist quoted above also says, "The charm and beauty of the wife at 25 are at the vanishing point." How was the author of the above statement able to infer that in 1938, when he wrote the piece, 20 percent of women were incapable of giving sexual satisfaction to their mates during their monthly period? Which medical paper, if any at all, validates such a statement? Nonetheless, suppose for a moment that the statistics presented by this writer are correct and medical science is fully in support of such a statement; the question remains, is it right to accept the institution of polygamy just because

20 percent of women are not able to give satisfaction to their mates for the few days of the month during their period? For the sake of argument, let us suppose that 20 percent of the female population are not able or are unwilling to have sexual intercourse with their husbands at all for the whole year. In civilized communities, even 20 percent would not justify passing a law that is detrimental to the entire female population.

Again, for the sake of argument, is it not also possible that 20 percent of men, due to excessive work, heavy-duty jobs, serving in the armed forces which takes them away from their homes, sickness, indifference, extramarital affairs, and last but not least, impotency, may be unable to give satisfaction to their wives? Should not the wives of the above ask for a law permitting polyandry?

The above-quoted apologist advocates polygamy because the husband would be able to get a young and presumably more attractive wife. But everyday experience proves that the age of twenty-five is not the "vanishing point" of a woman's charm and beauty. Some women, in fact, manifest their greatest appeal after their twenty-fifth year. Perhaps in a society where man is permitted to marry a girl when she is only nine or ten years old and have sex with her while she is still a minor, the beauty of such an ideal child-wife is thought to vanish quickly. For the rest of the world, where child-marriage is a crime and a nine- or ten-year-old girl is considered a child who belongs with her parents at home, it is hard to believe that a female loses her charm at twenty-five. In free and unorthodox societies, where laws prohibit child-marriage and girls can have the same freedom in education and careers as boys, the age of twenty-five is just the beginning of a long life. She can have her own profession, choose her own mate, take part in social activities, or settle down and rear the children while enjoying equality with her mate.

Polygamy in Islam Is an Improvement over an Ancient Arabian Custom

Muslim apologists contend that Islam permits polyg-amy because in pre-Islamic Arabia the number of wives that a man could acquire was unrestricted. Therefore, Islam adopted and improved upon a preexisting prac-tice by not allowing a man to marry more than four wives concurrently, and only if he could afford to sup-port them all equally:[11]

> Polygamy was practiced [in pre-Islamic Arabia] on an unlimited scale before the advent of Islam. Conse-quently, Islam did not abolish this deep-rooted prac-tice instantaneously to avoid a major social upheaval. In any case, polygamy is not peculiar to Islam.[12]

But as far as reliable evidence indicates, polygamy was *not* practiced in the major cities of Arabia. In Mecca, Muhammad's grandfather, uncle, and his own father were monogamists. His uncle, Abu Lahab, whose name is mentioned in the Koran, was also a monogamist:

> The Power of Abu Lahab will perish,
>   and he will perish.
> His wealth and gains will not exempt him.
> He will be plunged in flaming fire,

and his wife, the wood carrier,
will have upon her neck a halter of palm fibre.
(Koran 111: 1–5)

It was very clear from the above verse that Abu Lahab, who was very rich and could afford many wives, had only one.* Muhammad's powerful adversary, Abu Sufyan, who was the chief of the Quraysh (Muhammad's clan) and a very successful businessman, also had only one wife. Muhammad himself was a monogamist before he received his calling to Islam. The rest of his associates and close friends in Mecca were also monogamists.

As for Medina, we are almost certain that the people of that town were utterly against the polygamy before Islam. Gertrude Stern says:

> There is no reliable evidence of the practice of polygamy in pre-Islamic times at Al-Medina, as understood in the Islamic era, that is the system of a man marrying a number of women and maintaining them in one or more establishments. . . . Moreover, from a study of genealogical tables which I have compiled, it is to be observed that there is no indication of a well defined system of polygamy.[13]

Fatima Mernissi makes a similar point: "Another illustration is provided by the Ansar, the prophet's supporters. They thought polygamy so degrading that they

---

*His uncle's real name was 'Abd al-Uzza, "the slave of the goddess Uzza." His wife's name was Djumail. She was Abu Sufyan's sister, Muhammad's prominent adversary. She encouraged her husband to act against Muhammad.

forbade one of their daughters, Leila Bent Alkhatim, to marry the prophet."[14]

Even if we accept that polygamy was prevalent in pre-Islamic Arabia, it is difficult to believe that Muhammad would have been reluctant to do away with it if he had wanted to because of fear of social upheaval. As mentioned already, before Islam Arabs enjoyed drinking alcoholic beverages, especially wine. Yet, Muhammad banned intoxicating drinks totally, and everyone in Mecca, Medina, and every other part of the country eventually stopped drinking with some reluctance indeed, but without widespread social unrest.

By the same token Muhammad abolished prostitution without causing an uproar, despite the fact that prostitution had been a well-known fact of life in Mecca and other major cities. (A white banner on the top of the roof would indicate that women in that house were willing to "entertain" men for a price.)

The same point can be made about gambling. Arabs once enjoyed it, but then Muhammad called it a Satanic act and prohibited it; there was no resulting social upheaval. So, why did he not stop polygamy if indeed it had been practiced in the period? The answer is very simple: he liked sexual variety and could not confine himself to one woman. We don't really know whether he gambled or drank heavily because there is no proof either way. On the other hand, it is clear that some of his relatives and close associates regularly drank alcoholic beverages even after they embraced Islam. In fact, some of these people attended prayer services while drunk, as evidenced by the verse of the Koran: "O ye who believe! Draw not unto prayer when ye are drunken, till ye know that which ye utter." (4: 43)

The above verse was revealed at least sixteen years after Muhammad introduced Islam, "between the end of the third year and the end of the fifth year" after the Hegira.[15] A few years thereafter the use of intoxicating drinks was totally banned. "O ye who believe! Strong drink and games of chance and idols and divining arrows are only an infamy of Satan's handiwork. Leave it aside." (Koran 5: 90) This prohibition met with strong resistance, especially during the first five years of its restriction,[16] for the society was not prepared to abandon this popular pagan custom.

After Muhammad's death, the wine-drinking habit flourished anew. The Umayyad and 'Abbasid caliphs indulged in this greatly missed pleasure and prominent members of Islamic society followed suit, including even some members of the clergy.

In the years following the Prophet's death, some of his companions did not hesitate to let others know that they were not practicing abstinence. Early Muslim biographers tell us that these devoted associates of the Prophet tried to justify their wine-drinking habit with Koranic interpretations, even quoting a verse from the Islamic scripture. Abu Jaudad, for instance, a close companion of Muhammad who continued drinking, recited the following verse in response to his critics who pointed out to him that Muhammad had forbidden the habit: "There shall be no sin imputed unto those who believe and do good works for what they may have eaten." (Koran 5: 93)[17]

Some Muslim theologians thought that only wine was forbidden and that other alcoholic drinks did not fall under the prohibition. They even introduced a saying from the Prophet on the authority of Aisha, his wife, that he had said: "You may drink, but do not get drunk."[18] As already mentioned, there was a rumor that the Prophet himself used to drink *nabidh*, which is an intoxicating beverage made from dates or other fruits.[19]

On the other hand, the caliphs or jurists would sometimes take severe action against such misinterpretations of the law. It is reported that 'Umar, the second caliph and Muhammad's father-in-law, had some transgressors of the drinking ban flogged for their wrongdoing.[20]

But, Ma'mun, the famous 'Abbasid caliph who openly drank *nabidh*, declared, "I can not tolerate that a Qadi (judge) should drink Nabidh himself."[21]

Clearly there was a great deal of ambivalence and sometimes a double standard regarding beverages. A total prohibition against drinking never succeeded.

The point of this digression on drinking is to show that Muhammad did not shy away from imposing restrictions on even very popular customs. Similarly, even if polygamy had been a well-accepted practice in pre-Islamic Arabia, he could have made it illegal just as easily as he forbade wine-drinking. But, he did not declare polygamy unlawful because he was really in favor of it. The pattern of his own life shows that he wanted to have as many women as he could afford. That is why he made a special law for himself which gave him alone permission to marry as many women as he pleased (Koran 33: 59) even though he limited the number of wives for other Muslim men to only four, provided that they treat them with "equality and justice." (Koran 4: 3), for him, this condition of equality and justice was not binding.

But, when polygamy threatened to interfere with his

own daughter's happiness, Muhammad quickly reversed himself. Mernissi writes:

> Although he himself married thirteen women, he adamantly opposed 'Ali, his son-in-law, when the latter decided to contract a second marriage and thus provide Fatima, the prophet's favourite daughter (who did not marry as early as a pretty daughter should and who was not particularly known for her beauty), with an unwelcome co-wife.[22]

Al-Bukhari tells us that Allah's apostle said:

> I will not allow 'Ali Ibn Talib, and I repeat, I will not allow 'Ali to marry another woman except under the condition that he will divorce my daughter. She is a part of me and what harms her harms me.[23]

Here Muhammad implicitly admits that polygamy is, in fact, a serious cause of discord among cowives and destroys the happiness of the first wife. 'Ali remained a monogamist as long as Muhammad and his daughter lived. After their deaths, he practiced polygamy just as his Prophet and the rest of the true believers did.

Polygamy Can Only Be Practiced If Each Wife Is Ensured Just and Equal Treatment

Who is to judge that the man is treating his wives justly and equally if such treatment is left solely to the man's own conscience? In the Muslim community, the husband is supreme and his words and actions cannot be challenged by his wives. There is no way to find out that a polygamist is not treating his wives with equality and justice. There is no court in which injustice against a wife could be adjudicated; even if the man acknowledges the accusation, there is no punishment at all. Islamic jurisprudence records do not show a single case in which a man was ever tried and punished because he did not treat his wives equally.

Therefore, the condition of "treating wives with equality" is merely a deception and cannot be considered as a measure that restricts polygamy. Regarding the issue of fairness, Juliette Minces comments:

> The Koran maliciously adds that if the husband was not certain of his capacities in this regard (given that equity of this kind is probably impossible), then he should only take one wife, but the matter was left to his own conscience.[24]

When a man has absolute power over his wives and can divorce one or all of them with a single word, the number of the wives that a Muslim could have in his lifetime is practically unlimited and is bounded only by his caprice.

"The number of lawful wives," writes Muir, "is restricted to four; but these may at any moment be divorced at the caprice and by a simple word of the husband, and others substituted in their stead."[25]

The ideal woman, according to Muhammad, should be young, virginal, and ever obedient. This is clearly reflected in words he is reported to have said: "May it be yours to marry virgins, because their mouths are sweet, their wombs are prolific and they are more easily satisfied with little."[26] Again, when asked how a wife should be, he responded: "A woman who pleases him when he looks at her, obeys him when he commands, and does not oppose him in things which he regrets for her and himself."[27]

Polygamy Was Instituted to Encourage Marriage and Discourage Celibacy

Some Muslim fundamentalists agree that the Prophet promoted polygamy to encourage his male followers to get married as soon as possible, provided they could afford it. They maintain that Muhammad wanted to show that there is no celibacy in Islam and that polygamy was the answer to Christian monks and Manicheans, who preferred to stay away from marital life.

> The prophet, both by example and precept, encouraged the status of marriage. He positively endorsed marriage for all those who can afford it. And the well known saying [is] attributed to the prophet: There is no monkery in Islam.[28]

This is probably the weakest justification of all. Obviously, promoting monogamous marriages would also have discouraged celibacy.

CONCUBINAGE AND SLAVERY

> Concubinage may be defined as the more or less permanent cohabitation (outside the marriage bond) of a man with a woman or women, whose position would be that of secondary wives, women bought, acquired by gift, captured in war, or domestic slaves.[29]

Slavery, the main source of acquiring concubines, was recognized by Muhammad and was one of his methods of acquiring wealth. Since its endorsement in the Koran, slavery has never been abolished formally by any law. As we have seen, it is a matter of historical record that Muhammad and his followers captured women and children in raids who later were distributed among his men or sold in the slave markets.

Also, in the pre-Islamic period, Arabs frequently attacked one another's tribes in order to acquire young women. Muhammad, with his many raids of conquest, revitalized and perpetuated the old custom of slavery. There was no limit to the number of concubines a male Muslim might possess and no ceremony was needed to have sex with these bond women.

> As regards female slaves with whom (irrespective of his four wives) a Muslim may, without antecedent ceremony or any guarantee of continuance, co-habit, there is no limit.[30]

Theoretically, women slaves under Koranic law are merely "things, the property of their owners. The latter can alienate them as he likes, by sale, gift, dowry, or in other ways."[31] But, when a slave girl has borne a child to her master, she may not be disposed of, and at the death of her owner, she receives her freedom.[32] This Islamic law is a replica of an ancient Babylonian law, found on the famous Code of Hammurabi, which states: "After the father has gone to [his] fate, the children of the first wife and the children of the slave shall share equally in the goods of the parental estate."[33]

According to most experts, a male slave may have only two wives (half the entitlement of a free man). The slave may marry a slave girl or even a free woman if she consents. He must also pay her bride-price, but this price must be paid to the owner of the slave girl, not to the girl herself. The slaves can only marry with the consent of their masters.

It is illegal for a free man to actually marry his slave girls. He can, however, enjoy the master's privileges.[34] For example, it was common in some parts of India, before the Second World War, for a bride to take a number of girls to her husband's home, who "became the property, as it were, of the wife and husband."[35]

Aman Allah Khan, the deposed king of Afghanistan, had several pretty female slaves in his harem as recently as the 1920s. Some of the Muslims in Kashmir, before the Second World War, would marry four wives concurrently, take them across the border, sell them to the people of India, and return to repeat the same act again.

The phrase used for male or female slaves in Muhammad's scripture is "those whom your right hand possesses." Slavery is regarded in the Koran as Allah's established order. The masters of the slave women can, by Allah's ordinance, have sexual relations with them, whether they had been married or not at the time of captivity. "Unlawful for you are married women, except those whom your right hand possesses [slaves]." (Koran 4: 24) Women who are the booty of forays belong to the soldiers who took part in the raid. Many hundreds of thousands of women were captured by Muslims and were carried off. It did not matter if they were single or married, old women or children. Nor were these people ever entitled to any part of their masters' inheritance. The Koran enjoins: "Now those who are more favored will by no means hand over their provision to those [slaves] whom their right hands possess." (Koran 16: 71)

Apologists who desperately try to justify this barbaric institution argue that Muhammad could not have freed the slaves because: "The sudden and entire emancipation of the existing slaves was morally and economically impossible."[36] They also argue that Muhammad designed his laws of slavery in such a way that the institution could be eradicated entirely in the future. They claim that Muhammad himself was in favor of freeing the slaves, and quote the following words from him: "He who emancipates a Muslim slave, Allah will emancipate every member of his body from the fire, in return for the members (of his slaves)."[37]

But, the tradition quoted above does not seem to be authentic. If Muhammad had believed in the eventual emancipation of slaves, he would have set free his own slaves. At the time of his death, according to most reliable Muslim chroniclers, he owned at least fourteen slaves. Moreover, his followers did not seem to be aware of any intention to free the slaves on Muhammad's part (if in reality there was such an intention). The first caliph, Abu

Bakr, was the owner of several slaves. 'Umar, the second caliph, also owned more than thirty slaves. The number of slaves of the third caliph was more than forty.

As the Muslim empire expanded after the Prophet's death, the number of slaves acquired through conquest in Asia, Africa, and later Europe increased dramatically. Mu'tasim, the eighth 'Abbasid caliph of Baghdad, owned eight thousand slaves.[38]

Black as well as white slaves were annually imported by the thousands into the Muslim empire. In more recent times, Mecca, the birthplace of Muhammad, became the center of the slave trade.

Gradually, with increasing numbers, the slaves in the Muslim world became powerful. Uprisings broke out on occasion and, eventually, some slaves succeeded in forming a separate and independent Muslim dynasty (the Mamluk dynasty) in Egypt and other parts of the Arab world. The irony is that slavery and the slave-trade did not stop even after these revolts. In fact, it continued to grow, because it was believed to be a divine institution enjoined in the Koran and practiced by Muhammad as well as his successors. 'Umar made a rule that no Arab could be a slave, even if he were bought; only foreigners could be reduced to slavery.[39]

Slavery, therefore, was not only a common practice in Muhammad's time, but it increased beyond all expectation after the Prophet's death based on the words of the Koran and the deeds of Allah's Prophet. To quote from the Koran:

> Now, when ye encounter those who disbelieve, strike off their heads till you have made a great slaughter

among them, and of the rest, make fast the fetter and afterward either grace or ransom till the war lay down its burdens. That is the ordinance. (Koran 47: 4)

Stanley Lane Poole had this to say about these deplorable practices:

One cannot forget the unutterable brutalities inflicted on the conquered nations in taking the slaves. The Muslim soldier was allowed to do so as he pleased with any "infidel" woman he might meet on his victorious march. When one thinks of the thousands of women, mothers, and daughters, who must have suffered untold shame and dishonor by this he cannot find words to express his horror.[40]

The horrors of the Muslim slave-trade continued in the Middle East and North Africa right up to the beginning of the present century.

Through polygamy and concubinage, the male indulged his own sexual desires with no due consideration for the woman's sexual needs.[41] Polygamy prevents the development of any real love between a man and his wife. She is treated more or less as an agent rather than as a mate worthy of love and devotion. It devalues conjugal life, debases the family unit, and humiliates women.

Polygamy and concubinage may have once been suitable for the nomadic Arab tribes of the seventh century, but there is no justification whatsoever for these practices in a civilized society. Even the much more ancient matrimonial laws devised by the tyrant rulers of

Egypt, Babylonia, and Assyria were in many respects far superior to the later laws found in the Koran.

For example, in Babylonia, the aim of marriage was progeny. The wife could protect her status by bearing her husband children. If she was unable to have children, she had to provide her husband with a concubine who could bear him children. But a man was not allowed to take a second wife if his first wife was fertile or if the concubine offered by his wife could bear children. We quote from the famous code of Hammurabi (law 144):

> If a man marries a free woman, and she gives him a handmaid who bears children for her husband, he cannot marry another free woman.

Also of interest is law 145:

> If a man marries a free woman, and she cannot bear him children, and he decides to marry another wife, he can do so, and bring her into his house. But the second wife in no way is to be at the same level with the first wife.

Thus, only in this exceptional case, when the wife is barren, is the husband permitted to marry a second wife. The first wife cannot be cast off or repudiated because of her barrenness, and the position of the newcomer is inferior to the first wife. If the childless wife gives her husband a concubine who can provide him with progeny, he is not allowed the second marriage. The offering of a concubine by the legal wife to her husband is limited to one time only.

Clearly this ancient Babylonian law, promulgated by a "heathen" ruler who lived some twenty-four hundred years before Muhammad, is in every respect superior to the Koranic laws on polygamy.

We conclude this chapter with an anecdote regarding a learned Mullah who had *eight* wives in his harem—contrary to the limit of four stipulated in the Koran. He conveniently interpreted Koran 4: 3—"Marry of the women, who seem good to you, two or three or four"—by adding the numbers to produce a total of nine wives. Thus he was still entitled to one more![42]

4

ADULTERY AND
PUNISHMENTS FOR
SEXUAL MISCONDUCT

In Islam woman is considered to be the property first of her guardian (usually her father) and then ownership over her is transferred to her husband. This view of woman—as belonging at all times to some man—reflects a heavily male-dominant, patriarchal social system with ancient roots. Such a social system can be found all over the world and was especially prevalent at the earliest stages of history. In fact, according to Darwin, the same attitude is seen in many animal species. For example, a male ape who has several females in his possession will not permit any other male to approach them, even if the males are the offspring of his own females.[1]

Even among peoples where women have more influence than they do in Islam, any outside interference with female sexuality is usually seen as an infringement of a man's rights and arouses his jealousy. By the same token, adultery on the part of the woman is avenged by the man, who by this system of reasoning believes that his proprietary rights have been violated.[2]

The jealousy of the man naturally increases when he is permitted, as he is in Islam, to have more than one wife under contract, because he therefore has acquired more property to be defended against infringements from other men. Obviously women were kept in a state of subjugation under this social system and as a result any punishments meted out were always more severe for women than they were for men.

In this chapter we will look at the verses in the Koran dealing with sexual misconduct and discuss the punishments stipulated for each violation.

THE FIRST INJUNCTION: CONFINE LEWD WOMEN

> As for those of your women who are guilty of lewdness, call to witness four of you against them. And if they testify (to the truth of the allegation) then confine them to the houses until death take them or Allah appoint for them a way. (Koran 4: 15)

This is the first Koranic law revealed on the subject of adultery, which is presumably what the term "lewdness" refers to. According to the above ordinance, any woman who is proven to be unfaithful is to be confined to her house for the rest of her life. This life confinement, severe as it may seem, was perhaps considered light punishment for fornication in the opinion of Muhammad. As we will see in the following chapter, many Muslim women are not free to leave their quarters anyway. In some orthodox Muslim communities, women stay home all their lives and seldom venture out of the house except on very special occasions.

The law seems incomplete, however, because it does not provide any punishment for the man involved. Presumably in a male-dominant society he would be the aggressor, and yet he is permitted to live as before without even being questioned.

Muhammad's companions and close friends probably hinted at the incompleteness of the law to him and thus prompted him to change, or rather abrogate, it. Thus the second commandment given by Allah in this connection is much more strict and provides a prescribed punishment for both the man and the woman who have committed adultery.

THE SECOND INJUNCTION: SCOURGE THE ADULTERER AND ADULTERESS

The adulterer and adulteress, scourge ye each one of them (with) a hundred stripes. And let no pity for the twain withhold you from obedience to Allah, if you believe in Allah and the Last Day. And let a party of believers witness their punishment. (Koran 24: 2)

Depending on the physical strength of the executioner and his zeal for inflicting punishment, a flogging of one hundred lashes would sometimes result in the death of the condemned. More often than not, this sort of savage punishment caused both culprits, especially the woman, to be crippled forever. Flogging can also result in severe internal injuries.

In the Islamic courts, which are supervised by a member of the clergy, the Mullah, there is no right of the accused to defend themselves. As soon as the four witnesses render their testimonies, the judge will give the predetermined verdict and the executioner then carries out the sentence to the letter. There is no defense counsel.

There is also no minimum or maximum punishment or any option in between. Even the judge is not free to decide between the maximum or minimum sentence, nor is he free to pronounce the sentence in a way that he thinks is appropriate as a human being. In other words, the judge is not free to render a judgment. The law is made by Allah and no one dares to defy or change it. When the court accepts the testimonies of the four witnesses, the verdict is already known, and it stands at one hundred stripes, no more and no less.

This law by itself reflects the barbarity of an ancient patriarchal system, which probably dates back to pre-Islamic days. The woman is brutally treated and her paramour is savagely flogged. Someone has trespassed upon a man's private property and so his rights must be satisfied through punishment of the offenders.

Note the second line. If you are a true believer in Allah and faithful to Islam, you should not show any

sign of compassion or mercy. Although Allah is repeatedly described in the Koran as "the compassionate and
merciful," by modern standards his justice is very cruel.
In fact, many passages of the Koran describe him in
quite a different light. He is the avenger: "Allah is
mighty, able to requite" (Koran 3: 4); Allah plots against
his own creation, against his people: "And they [the dis-
believers] plotted, and Allah plotted [against them]:
Allah is the best of the plotters" (Koran 3: 54); Allah pun-
ishes very severely, his revenge proves fatal: "Lo! Thy
Lord . . . is owner of dire punishment" (Koran 41: 43; see
also 2: 165; 2: 196; 2: 211; 3: 11; 5: 2, 98; 8: 13, 25, 48, 52; 13:
6; 40: 3, 22; 59: 4, 7); "Thy Lord is swift in prosecution"
(Koran 6: 166; 7: 167); "He is powerful to revenge: He is
omnipotent over His slaves." (Koran 6: 18)

Following these Koranic depictions of the Almighty,
no Islamic judge would dare to have mercy on the accused. Allah's law is rigid and the sentence is inflexible.
There is no appeal from the sentence either. A judgment
rendered in the seventh century for the desert nomads
must be rendered in the same way at the end of the twentieth century without any improvement or alteration.

The final line of this second injunction stipulates that
the flogging must be carried out in public and in the presence of the faithful: "And let a party of believers witness
their punishment." The intent is obviously to deter others
from wrongdoing. A public flogging is a most humiliating
punishment not only for those under sentence, but for
their kinfolk, friends, and relatives, who had no part in the
"crime." All of their kin share in the anguish of the punishment. Apparently, this barbaric law aims to destroy the
root of love that binds family and friends together.

Muslim jurisprudents and apologists hold that only through such laws, "handed over to" Muhammad by Allah, can Muslim communities, or any other community for that matter, be cleaned of evils. They argue that if the Koranic law is carried out to the letter in each Muslim country, there would be no more crime.

A little research will reveal the hypocrisy of this contention. A good deal of lewdness goes on in Muslim countries with orthodox laws, but it is never uncovered. As long as lovers keep a low profile and conceal their love affairs, they are safe—when there is no witness, there is no trial, therefore no conviction. Extramarital affairs have not stopped altogether among even very orthodox Muslim people.

STONING

It was pointed out in the preceding sections that according to separate verses of the Koran (4: 15 and 24: 2) adultery should be punished either by house confinement or by a hundred lashes administered in public. Adding to this confusion is a tradition that maintains the punishment for adultery was later changed to stoning of both the adulterer and the adulteress.[3] It is said that Muhammad replaced the punishments specified in the Koran with stoning, which is believed to have been derived from Judaism (Deut. 23: 22; Lev. 19: 20).

After Muhammad died, a difference of opinion emerged among the believers. Most of them maintained that the Koran plainly and explicitly abrogates the sentence of stoning. But 'Umar, whose personality was very dominating among the faithful, argued that the Prophet had ordained stoning of adulterers. Being Muhammad's father-in-law, close associate, and the second caliph, he eventually silenced the dispute and favored the traditional accounts of the deeds of the Prophet (sunna) against the text of the Koran.

Another theory holds that the injunction of stoning had been originally a part of chapter thirty-three, but this is doubtful.

One can clearly see that there was some confusion of mind on the part of Muhammad regarding the seriousness of this transgression. At first he decides to enjoin house confinement of the woman alone. Then he changes his mind and commands flogging of both parties involved. If we are to believe traditions outside of the Koran, he later changed the punishment to stoning. Such confusion makes it next to impossible for the objective reader to accept the Koran as the inerrant word of God.

In any case, Muslim jurisprudence applies both punishments. It draws a distinction between two types of adultery, the latter being more serious:

1. An extramarital affair of a man with a woman who is not married to someone else. Scourging is administered for this lesser transgression.

2. An extramarital affair of a man with a married woman. Death by stoning is the penalty in this case.

The transgression is established in two different ways in the Islamic court: either the accused admits the crime personally and makes a confession or proof of the deed is presented to the court.

In the first instance, the court procedure is simply an

automatic decision-making process. The judge, after hearing the confession, establishes the fact that the accused is a legal adult and of sound mind, and asks the accused if he (she) really considers himself (herself) to be a violator of the Koranic law. If the answer is affirmative each time it is asked, the crime is established as a fact in the eyes of the law and the sentence is pronounced accordingly.

In the second instance, when the accused is brought before the court, Islamic law calls for four eyewitnesses "who are able to confirm the truth of the accusation in detail."[4] They must swear that they have seen the actual penetration. The requirement of four male witnesses is enjoined in the Koran: "Produce four witnesses from among you against them." (Koran 24: 13) Although it may seem improbable that four witnesses could prove that they actually saw the penetration of the woman by the man, if they swear to it, their evidence must be credited, and the judge cannot reject it. This act of infringing upon someone else's privacy and spying on the bedroom of a neighbor or friend is thus compatible with and in some ways encouraged by Islamic laws.

Usually these four witnesses are required to be male, but if it is not possible to produce four male witnesses, then three male and two female testimonies are considered just as valid, i.e., two women witnesses in lieu of one man. This is the only combination acceptable in Islamic court. This does not, however, mean that for every male, two females could testify. The law accepts a total of only two women witnesses, no more. This is another patent example of the way in which woman in Islam is treated as the inferior sex.

The mode of execution for those found guilty of

adultery, according to tradition and Islamic law, is unbelievably cruel and barbaric.

After the sentence for stoning to death is issued by the judge, the woman is taken out of the court to a public place to give the curious the opportunity to view the execution. A hole is dug for her and she is placed in it in a standing position. The hole is then filled in with dirt so that she won't be able to move.

The four eyewitnesses come forward and approaching her in this helpless position, each throws a stone at her. Next the judge takes part in this savage act, hurling a stone at her from the prepared "ammunition of death." Finally, every one of the Muslim bystanders joins in the show, pelting the miserable creature with stones.

It is indeed a show of savagery. A helpless, panicked woman, buried in a grave in an upright position, is murdered by a frenzied crowd of zealots, some of whom joyfully compete to inflict the most terrible injuries upon the wretched soul. And all of this is fully sanctioned by law. In the last seven years, at least four cases of this barbaric punishment have been implemented in the Islamic Republic of Iran alone.

This method of stoning reportedly goes back to Muhammad himself, as once he ordered a hole to be dug for an Arab woman named Ghamdiya who was accused of adultery.[5] 'Ali, his cousin and son-in-law, who succeeded him as the fourth caliph, tried another woman accused of fornication and condemned the girl, Shuraha Hamdiani, to be stoned to death exactly in the same manner as the Prophet had done some thirty years before. Since accounts of Muhammad's deeds are the main source of jurisprudence next to the Koran, 'Umar, 'Ali, and all the other Muslim jurists and rulers had no other alternative but to follow the example of the Prophet.

There is no specific rule for stoning a man. Apparently, based on a tradition of Muhammad, when he sentenced a man named Maiz to be stoned, he did not clarify the mode of execution. We quote from a reliable and authentic Muslim jurisprudence text on the subject of execution by stoning:

> It is necessary, when a whoremonger is to be stoned to death, that he should be carried to some barren place void of houses and cultivation, and it is requisite that the stoning be executed first by witnesses and after them by the Imam or Qadi [religious leader or judge], and after those by the rest of the bystanders, because it is so recorded from 'Ali [Muhammad's cousin], and also because in the circumstances of the execution, begun by the witnesses, there is a precaution, since a person may be very bold in delivering his evidence against a criminal, but afterwards, when directed himself to commence the infliction of the punishment which is a consequence of it, [he] may from compunction retract his testimony; thus, causing the witness to begin the punishment may be a means of entirely preventing it. [The Muslim apologists do not explain, however, that if the witnesses who accuse a man are his antagonists and through perjury maliciously conspire to convict him, then there is no one who could stop the execution.]

When a woman is to be stoned, a hole or excavation should be dug to receive her, as deep as her waist, because the Prophet ordered such a hole to be dug for Ghamdiyah before mentioned, and 'Ali also ordered a hole to be dug for Shuraha Hamdiani. . . . It is laudable to dig a hole for her, as decency is thus most effectually preserved. There is no manner of necessity to dig a hole for a man, because the Prophet did not do so in the case of Maiz.[6]

According to the above report, it was Muhammad himself who enjoined the savage law of stoning in Islam, and it was also he who devised the barbaric way of carrying out the sentence.

DISCRIMINATION AGAINST WOMEN IN PENAL LAWS

The inequality of man and woman in Islam is seen even in the mode of their punishment. In regard to stoning, the woman is buried in a standing position up to her waist (really her breasts)—under the pretext of preserving public decency—and cannot move at all, much less cover her head and face to avoid the barrage of deadly stones. But the convicted man is free to move around, cover his head and face with both arms, and even run for his life, as anyone in that situation would do. She experiences a more bitter and horrible death.

Islamic law enjoins that even a condemned sick woman must be put to death immediately. There is no moratorium in such cases. Muslim theologians maintain that since the adulteress must be destroyed anyway, as Muhammad ordained, there is no justification for delay.

In certain Islamic schools, a woman convicted of fornication receives a double punishment: first, she is scourged with a hundred lashes as specified in Koran 24: 2, and then she is stoned to death in the manner explained before. Many scholastic minutiae are presented by different sects. The Shiites, one of the fanatical Muslim sects, advocate this double punishment for fornication. They also maintain that if a married woman (*muhsan*) has sexual intercourse with a minor boy, she should receive a hundred lashes only; but if she cohabits with an adult man who is mentally imbalanced and is not her husband, then she should be stoned to death without scourging.[7] Discrimination against woman is manifested here also. If a man has sexual intercourse with a teenaged girl or an insane woman, he is sentenced to one hundred lashes only and not stoning.

If a man has divorced his wife by means of the irrevocable repudiation of triplicate divorce (to be discussed later), and then is caught with the divorced wife in bed, both of them will be stoned to death. It may seem astonishing, but it is true!

If a man commits the act of sodomy with a woman other than his wife, according to the Hanafi school (which comprises the largest number of believers), he is to be corrected by scourging.[8] But sodomizing one's own wife, even without her consent, is permitted in Islam, because the Koran enjoins: "Your women are (like) a tilled field for you, so enter into your tilled field any way you please." (Koran 2: 223)

Obviously there is very little systematic consistency to these penal laws. A man who sodomizes a woman who is not his wife gets away with a lesser punishment than a man who sleeps with his divorced wife. The former is scourged while the latter is stoned to death!

There are many other examples of such inconsistencies and inequalities:

If a Muslim man commits adultery with a nonbeliever's wife in a non-Muslim land or in the territory of Islam where the populace revolted against their government, he is not to be stoned.

If a man who had confessed to adultery is able to run to safety during the execution process, the process must stop. This opportunity to escape not only can save his life, but his former confession is considered thereby nullified.[9] A woman, on the other hand, could never escape her punishment because she is buried up to her waist in a hole and unable to run to safety. Even if she decides to deny her confession of adultery, there is no reprieve from the execution sentence.

If a man cohabits with a slave girl of his son or grandson, there is no punishment for him. However, if a woman has sexual relations with a male slave of her daughter or granddaughter, she will be punished accordingly.

Strangely, under certain penal laws, slaves are better off than free persons. For example, slaves are not stoned for adultery or fornication. They are flogged, but with only fifty lashes. This too follows the Koran: ". . . then if they [the slave girls] are guilty of adultery when they are taken in marriage, they shall suffer half the punishment (prescribed) for free women." (Koran 4: 25)

Having sexual relations with an unmarried woman calls for chastising both parties by flogging. In order to implement the punishment, the man's clothing is taken off except for his underwear (slip), his hands are tied to a pole or a tree, and he is then flogged in a standing position. The woman, on the other hand, is scourged in a sitting position with her veil wrapped around her body. This mode of scourging for the man and the woman is attributed to 'Ali, Muhammad's cousin, who reportedly said: "Correction is to be inflicted upon a man standing and upon a woman sitting." In Islamic jurisprudence "correction" means scourging, of course. Scourging is practiced today in Muslim countries with orthodox governments: Saudi Arabia, Pakistan, Sudan, and Iran.

These are but a few examples of many such inhumane punishments.

CALIPHS ARE ABOVE THE LAW

Of course, for the supreme ruler there was no punishment and no accountability to the law. When the caliph or his standing jurisprudent committed a felony, such as bribery, theft, fornication, or even rape and murder, no one could prosecute him. With the exception of a handful of caliphs a great number of Muslim rulers indulged in sexual intercourse outside of their overfilled harems, and they even had incestuous and unlawful sexual relations with their blood relatives.

Drunkenness was also a frequent weakness of many caliphs. Most of the Umayyid caliphs were often drunk, even during prayer time.

Regarding sexual transgressions, there are some notorious examples. Harun al-Rashid, the great 'Abbasid caliph, slept with his own sister. Ma'mun, his son, who ruled the western part of the vast Muslim empire, cohabited with his aunt. Khalid Walid, the commander of the Muslim army under the first caliph, Abu Bakr, killed a chieftain in a most treacherous way in order to possess the man's wife for himself. She was very pretty and the commander had developed a strong sexual desire for her. When Abu Bakr was told what his army commander had done, the caliph would not prosecute Khalid because, he said, he was nicknamed the "sword of Allah" (*saif Allah*) by the Prophet and he could do nothing against Allah's sword!

But the wives of these high-ranking Muslim officials were not exempted from punishment like their mates. For according to Koran 4: 34: "Men are in charge of women, because Allah hath made the one of them to excel the other."

FALSE ALLEGATIONS AND OATHS

Sometimes the husband may accuse his wife of infidelity based solely on jealousy. If he cannot prove that his wife was unfaithful by providing four just witnesses, his punishment is eighty lashes for slander. In order to avoid the prescribed punishment of flogging, he must repeat his allegation four times and each time take an oath to Allah that he is telling the truth.

> As for those who accuse their wives but have no witnesses except themselves; let the testimony of one of

them be four testimonies, (swearing) by Allah that he is of those who speak the truth; and yet a fifth, invoking the curse of Allah on him if he speaketh not the truth. (Koran 24: 6, 7)

Against this allegation there is only one avenue open to the wife to defend herself. She, in turn, can also swear that she is innocent and her husband is not telling the truth. In other words, when a man, filled with jealousy or malevolence, accuses his wife of adultery without producing four witnesses, she can defy his allegation by taking an oath and swearing four times that the accusation is false. In this connection, the Koran states:

And it shall avert the punishment from her if she bear witness before Allah four times that the thing he said is indeed false. And a fifth (time) that the wrath of Allah be upon her, if he speaketh the truth. (Koran 24: 8–9)

Swearing by a deity to back up one's statement was an old custom among the nomadic Arabs. It did not start with the Arabs and was a prevalent technique among many ancient peoples thousands of years before Muhammad. In this particular case, when a man accuses his wife of sexual relations with another, there are some very striking similarities between the injunction of the Koran and the Code of Hammurabi from ancient Babylon (circa 1790 B.C.E.), which we mentioned previously (chapters 2 and 3). Hammurabi's law was copied and sent to different parts of his empire and was later translated into different languages, becoming the basis of many civil laws of the ancient world. The Arabian peninsula, especially its northern section, could not have been out of the influence of the code; so it is not unreasonable to assume that it influenced Arab legal tradition, which was later adapted by Muhammad. When we compare the Koran with the Code of Hammurabi regarding the allegation of infidelity, we find that, according to the Babylonian law, any husband who suspects his wife of infidelity could not have punished her without proof: "If a man's wife has been accused by her husband, but she has not been caught lying with another male, she shall swear by a god and return to her home."[10]

Despite a time difference of about twenty-three centuries, the two laws regarding the slandering of a wife are almost identical. It therefore stands to reason that Muhammad perpetuated an old established law, which can be traced all the way back to Babylon.

Nonetheless, in spite of the similarities of the two laws, there are some good points in the Code of Hammurabi, which make it much more liberal to an open-minded student. Let us compare the law of allegation in both documents and look at the merits and shortcomings of each.

1. Koranic law 24: 8 requires the wife who is accused of infidelity by her husband to "bear witness before Allah four times" in order to avert the danger of harsh punishment, whereas the Code of Hammurabi (law 131) requires the wife to swear only one oath.

2. Koranic law stipulates that the accused wife must swear by Allah, god of Islam. But if the wife is a nonbeliever or non-Muslim, swearing to Allah does not have a real meaning and the oath is useless. In Hammurabi's law,

the wife could take an oath by "a god," any god she respects, not necessarily her husband's god. Apparently, the Babylonian law establishes a mode of freedom in beliefs.

3. In accordance with the Koranic injunction (24: 9), after the wife takes the oath by Allah four times, she is required to call on Allah a fifth time to curse her if she is a liar. However, there is no such sanction for her husband, who may have mistakenly or maliciously accused his wife of infidelity. Here the woman is humiliated because it is she who has to apologize indirectly by imploring Allah to curse her if she is not telling the truth. Her defense is questioned even though the accusation remains unproven. In Hammurabi's law, the accused wife does not have to go through the mental agony of begging the god to curse her. She does not have to prove anything. Obviously, neither of these laws would meet modern Western standards. But if a woman of any civilized society today were compelled to choose one of them, she would probably prefer the Babylonian law to that of the Koran.

FALSE ACCUSATION AND THE CONTROVERSY SURROUNDING AISHA'S FIDELITY

And those who accuse honorable women but bring not four witnesses, scourge them (with) eighty stripes and never (afterwards) accept their testimony. They indeed are evil doers. (Koran 24: 4)

Commentators on the Koran tell us that the above passage was revealed in response to those people who doubted the chastity of one of Muhammad's youngest and prettiest wives, Aisha. In chapter 1 we related the circumstances that led to Aisha being left behind Muhammad's caravan one night. The next day she rejoined her husband with the help of a young man named Safwan ibn al-Mu`attal. Her disappearance and then reappearance with the young man gave rise to malicious rumors about infidelity and much consternation on Muhammad's part. The episode took place in the fifth year of the Hegira when Aisha was only thirteen and Muhammad was returning from the campaign against the tribe of Banu al-Mustaliq.

This is how Aisha told her side of the story:

> When Safwan passed me, he had fallen behind the main body for some purpose and had not spent the night with the troops. He saw my form and came and stood over me. He used to see me before the veil was prescribed for us, so when he saw me, he exclaimed in astonishment, "The apostle's wife!" He asked what had kept me behind, but I did not speak to him. Then, he brought up his camel and told me to ride it while he kept behind. So, I rode it and he took the camel's head going forward quickly in search of the army, and by Allah, we did not overtake them and I was not missed until the next morning.[11]

. . . .

> Then the army halted and while they were resting, the man came up leading me. Then the liars said what they do say, and the army was in a state of turmoil.[12]

The people who saw the young camel driver, Safwan, with Muhammad's youngest wife were at first astonished and later started to gossip, accusing Aisha of infidelity.

> The scandal loving Arabs were not slow in drawing sinister conclusions from the inopportune situation and spread the word abroad. The estrangement of Muhammad from his favorite wife strengthened the grounds of defamation.[13]

Muhammad, in his distress, did not know what to do. Although he was burning with anger and jealousy, he was very attached to his child-wife and did not want to part with her—after all, she was his favorite.

Muhammad apparently questioned his wife's fidelity as well because she was sent to her parents' house. As he could not and did not want to lose her, and he could not stop the tattling tongues of his followers, he asked the advice of some of his close associates. A variety of opinions were presented. His cousin, 'Ali, told him to divorce her and get rid of the scandal. Some Islamic writers maintain that Muhammad's youngest daughter, Fatima, who was married to 'Ali and very jealous of Aisha because she had attracted the affection of her father and taken her deceased mother's place, encouraged her husband, 'Ali, to present the harshest solution: "Divorce her! There are plenty of young and beautiful girls who would be more than willing to marry you."[14]

As always, he referred the matter to Allah, who came to his aid by giving him the following verse:

Lo! They who spread the slander are a gang among
    you. Deem it not a bad thing for you;
nay, it is good for you. Unto every man of them (will
    be paid) that which he hath earned
of the sin; and as for him among them who had the
    greater share therein, his will be an
awful doom. Why did not the believers, men and
    women, when ye heard it, think good of
their own folk, and say: it is a manifest untruth? Why
    did they not produce four witnesses?
Since they produce not witnesses, they verily are liars
    in the sight of Allah.

                              (Koran 24: 11–13)

It is said by most historians and biographers of Muhammad that there were especially two men in Medina, named Hassan and Mistah, who were responsible for spreading rumors of Aisha's infidelity. Basing his actions on the Koran, Muhammad ordered his soldiers to seize the two men and inflicted on them the Koranic punishment—eighty lashes each. A woman named Hamma also received the same punishment. She was the sister of Zaynab (Muhammad's wife) who, perhaps out of pure jealousy, was Aisha's ardent antagonist and adversary. After such a severe punishment, the slanderers were quieted and the gossip died down.

Aisha once more resumed her role as the Prophet's favorite wife and she kept that position in his harem for the next five years until he died.

There is, however, another side to this story which throws a shadow of doubt over the whole episode, especially Aisha's chastity. According to a great many Islamic historians, the above incident occurred when Muhammad was triumphantly returning from a campaign against the Banu Mustaliq tribe. Recall from chapter 1 that it was after this expedition that Muhammad acquired a new wife named Juwayriyya, to whom Aisha took an instant dislike because of her beauty.

During the honeymoon Muhammad apparently must have neglected Aisha, who was accompanying him on the expedition. Polygamy always has its ill effects. Perhaps Aisha, feeling forsaken, tried to have a little fun for herself with a young, good-looking man who was in the same expedition. There are a number of factors that make this interpretation of the events probable:

1. At the time of the episode, Muhammad was in his late fifties and Aisha, at thirteen, was on the crest of teenage passion and feelings. The Prophet's attention was divided among his various military expeditions, social activities, and cohabitation with a dozen wives. It would not be unnatural for a young girl like her under these circumstances to search for a paramour as her husband did so often.

2. According to Aisha herself, she knew the young camel driver before the order of the veil was imposed; therefore, they were not meeting for the first time.

3. The history writers tell us that because Aisha was very small and thin, the man in charge of her litter did not notice, or rather did not feel, her absence when he lifted the litter onto the camel's back. It is difficult to accept this childish reasoning. The man in charge of the litter could easily have detected that it was empty from the lack of sounds from within. It is true that the order of the veil would have prevented his seeing his mistress's

face, but he was not barred from talking to her to know if she felt comfortable or needed anything. In fact, the Koran specifically allows such conversation: "When you ask of them [the wives of the Prophet] anything, ask it of them from behind a curtain." (Koran 33: 53) How is it possible that Aisha's attendant did not become aware that his mistress was missing the entire night?

4. It is reported that Aisha arrived at Muhammad's headquarters the next day with the young camel driver leading the camel. How could her husband not have known that she was missing that night and even part of the next day until she arrived? Muhammad had taken Aisha with him on this expedition so that he might have the pleasure of her company during the journey. Perhaps Aisha disappeared when Muhammad was preoccupied with Juwayriyya.

5. When a camel bearing a litter is brought up to the door of a tent or house, it is made to kneel down until the passenger enters the litter. During this time, the curtain of the litter is drawn to one side to allow the rider in. As soon as the traveler is inside the litter, she herself or her attendants draw the curtain, the sign that she is ready to move along. Then the camel stands up and proceeds. The man in charge of Aisha's litter could not have failed to notice that the curtain was not drawn and that she was not inside.

6. According to the biographers, after this incident, Muhammad quarreled with his wife. He was angry with her and afterwards would not talk to her. She fell ill from sorrow and his indifference. Later, she was sent to her parents. Her father, Abu Bakr (literally: "father of the virgin"), spoke with his son-in-law about the divorce of his

daughter. Aisha stayed one month in her parent's home and Muhammad refused to sleep with her for that time.

7. By Aisha's own account, Safwan recognized her without difficulty because he had seen her before Muhammad's wives were forced to wear the veil. She also says she did not talk to him. If she was wearing her veil, how could he have known her in the middle of the night in the Arabian desert without any light? Does not this part of the story seem a bit strange?

8. It is curious that of all the followers of Muhammad the man who was assigned to follow the caravan and pick up the strays or missing items was a young, handsome camel driver of twenty-four who had known Aisha before the order of the veil was imposed.

9. The allegation of the infidelity of Aisha was mainly made by close relatives of Muhammad himself: his daughter, Fatima; his cousin, 'Ali; and his sister-in-law, Hammam. They should have had his interests at heart.

10. It is reported by some writers that because of this episode, Safwan did not receive the same attention from Muhammad any more. Some even believe that he was mysteriously killed in one skirmish. Thus, the man on whose account fifteen verses of the Koran were revealed disappeared quietly from the scene of Islamic history without further trace.

Based on the aforementioned points, it is not unreasonable to conclude that there may have been some truth to the rumor of Aisha's infidelity. Muhammad himself probably suspected as much, but he was also aware that he could not stay away from his beloved child-wife, the only woman who had offered her virginity to him. Let us not forget that virginity of the woman was a very important factor in marriage among the Arabs.

In any case, with the Koranic law stipulating that four eyewitnesses were necessary to prove an adulterous love affair, Muhammad was able to put an end to the rumors of his wife's infidelity. Clearly, no one could furnish four men who would testify that they had seen the act of sexual intercourse between Safwan and Aisha, especially since their encounter took place in the middle of the night and in the vast, isolated space of the desert. Thus Aisha's status in the harem was restored and her accusers were punished with eighty lashes, as the law also commands.[15]

5

THE VEIL AND
WOMAN'S SECLUSION

One of the most controversial Islamic laws with respect to women is the requirement for complete veiling in accordance with Koranic tenets. The Muslim clergy, theologians, and fundamentalist believers argue that, on the basis of passages in the Koran and the tradition of Muhammad himself, a woman should not be permitted to leave her house in the first place, and if she has to go out, she must shroud herself in a loose garment, cover her hair, and must not reveal any ornaments or make-up that she may have used. Most of the jurisconsults of the Islamic world maintain that a woman should not leave her house and go into the streets unless it is absolutely necessary. She is excluded from outdoor activities and is lodged in special quarters, segregated from all men except those closest to her, such as her father, brother, and husband.

The wearing of the veil was instituted by Muhammad in the early days of Islam. Within about one hundred years of his death, the institution of veiling and seclusion had been spread all over the Middle East by invading Muslims in pursuit of plunder from the once rich and independent countries of that region: "One and a half centuries after the death of the prophet, the system was fully established, with all the appurtenances of the harem, in which amongst the richer classes, the women were shut off from the rest of the household under the charge of eunuchs."[1]

The use and significance of the veil have gone through many different phases and interpretations in the course of Islamic history. One of the most orthodox Islamic schools, the Hanbali in Baghdad, objects to the appearance of women in the streets even if they are veiled. The followers of this school firmly maintain that no woman should ever be seen outside the home.

One Egyptian caliph ordered all the women in his empire to stay in their houses, and no woman was ever permitted to go in the streets. He took pride in this instruction and boasted that he was restoring the original Islamic practice. According to him, the veiling of women meant their complete confinement and seclusion. Many Western travelers' accounts show that even as late as the turn of the century, noble women in Egypt were proud of not having left their houses after marriage. It is also reported that an Egyptian caliph ordered the manufacture of ladies' shoes to be stopped so that no woman could leave her house and go outside.

The complete seclusion of woman in some Islamic countries of Asia is called *purdah,* a Persian word meaning curtain or veil as well as privacy and seclusion. In practical terms, it means the total veiling of women from head to foot when they are outside the home and the segregation of males from females in the house. A great majority of Muslim women in fundamentalist countries, whether in Asia or Africa, the two most predominant Muslim continents, practice the law of veiling and seclusion. And every Muslim male considers it a religious command to have his close female relatives cover themselves completely.

For generations women in Islam have submitted with little complaint or protest to the Koranic rule of the veil. The law is very rigid and very few women, in the long history of Islam, have dared to defy it. In fact, at the turn of the last century, almost all Muslim females used the veil. "One can generalize," says Jones, "without fear of inaccuracy of saying that at least 95% of Muslim women, perhaps even more, observe purdah constantly and logically."[2] The figure may not be that high in Muslim communities today because the validity and usefulness of the veil were challenged in the 1930s in countries like Turkey and Iran, where purdah was then officially abolished. Unfortunately, there are places like Pakistan, the Persian Gulf states, and some North African communities where the seclusion of women is rigorously observed by the inflexible laws of the governments and severe punishment is prescribed for those who do not comply with the Koranic rule.

THE WILL OF ALLAH VS. CRIES FOR EMANCIPATION

The inflexible laws of Islam have deprived half of the population of their equal rights. The male is in charge of the female (Koran 4: 34) and the subjugated half is led to believe, through Islamic teachings, that the supremacy of the man is the will of Allah and it has been predestined for women to live as submissive, obedient wives. They have been forced to accept that women are inferior to men; that their testimony is equal to only half that of the man; that they should inherit one-half of the male share from the deceased; that Allah does not want to see any woman unveiled in the street; that she may not converse with men except her father or brother; that any conversation with a man other than her close kin should be carried out from behind a curtain; and that woman is not supposed to have a position or a job in which men would be working for her and take direct orders from her. The only job for her is to be secluded at home, preparing the food, washing the clothing, and keeping her husband's bed warm.

The majority of Muslim women are brought up with the conviction that it is Allah's command for them to be under male dominance. Their fates are interwoven with that of their men. They accept their inferiority without any regret or malice. Jones says, "The pitiable thing is that the great majority accept the seclusion with a kind of fatal resignation, explaining anything and everything to their satisfaction with such a remark as 'It is our custom,' 'It is our fate,' 'It is our religion.' "[3]

Yet the Muslim clergy and jurisprudents are disturbed over the cries of equality between the sexes heard among educated Muslim women who believe that the rising tide of modernism will eventually triumph over the prejudices of the Dark Ages. The apologists know that if they don't protect the Koranic law of the veil, segregation, and women's seclusion against the liberal minds of the opposition, the institutions of polygamy and purdah will be abolished. As a result, their indisputable positions as the supreme guardians of Allah's ordinance will be at stake. For this and similar reasons, they present such views as the following: "Man and women are like fire and cotton whose meeting together is always destructive."[4]

Other apologists try to base their arguments against the liberation of women on observations of modern science. The faithful are led to believe that the inequality of male and female is based on their apparent physical differences. Proponents maintain that women's inferiority is genuine and natural because of the way she is created, especially in regard to menstruation, pregnancy, child birth, and breast feeding. They regard all these natural phenomena as signs of inferiority. The Muslim clergy hold that the male, being the stronger, should prevail and the female, being the weaker sex, therefore must be subordinate. These arguments are obviously specious and have little relevance to modern society, where the determinants of progress are mental factors such as intellectual ability, talent, drive, and education, not physical strength or the temporary indispositions of the female reproductive system.

THE MAZE OF RESTRICTIONS AGAINST WOMEN

In orthodox Muslim countries today every aspect of life is regulated to ensure strict segregation of the sexes. This separation is observed both in public and private life. In some countries, the women are separated from the men even on public transportation. It was shown in the preceding chapter how Aisha was left behind in the desert one night all by herself. According to the story, the man in charge of the litter of Muhammad's favorite wife claimed not to know whether she was in her carefully curtained box because he was never allowed to view her.

Of course, today's system of transportation is quite different from what it was during the time of Allah's apostle. Instead of camels and litters, cars and buses are standard. Nonetheless, the old style of seclusion of the women is more or less preserved: bus and train compartments provide separate seats and areas for women that conceal them from the gazes of male travelers.[5] In some of the oil-rich Arab countries, the private cars of the well-to-do families are curtained and severe punishment is meted out to any inquisitive outsiders who try to look inside the cars.

In places where women are not permitted to drive a car, middle-class women must ask their husbands or close male relatives to give them a ride. The lower class of women must take public transportation, which, as has been mentioned, has a special closed section for them.

When a woman leaves her house to go shopping or to visit her folks, she is to veil herself completely. The garment she uses for veiling is different in the various Muslim communities. In North Africa she wears what is called a *burqa*. This is a long garment, usually black, covering the entire body of the woman from head to foot. There are two holes in the headcover for the woman's eyes. Fine embroidery or netting ornament these holes. In this way the woman is able to see where she is going but no one can see her eyes, much less her face.

> The old style burqa is perhaps the most effective means of concealing a woman, for it consists of a circular piece of material with its center intricately embroidered to create a skull cap, which drops right down to the garment around the woman, giving a rather ghostly impression. The effect of all these garments is the same, though; for the woman is rendered anonymous, a non-person, unapproachable, just a silent being skulking along, looking neither to the right or left. To those who do not know her personally, she is nameless and faceless.[6]

A woman wearing such a horrible garment is not only a nameless prisoner in the street, but she is a taboo. No one dares talk to her or even ask a simple question lest her close male kin get suspicious and cause trouble. The faceless creature is doomed to wear such a garment whenever she enters the street.

We might describe the burqa as the combination of the early Islamic headcover mentioned in Koran 33: 59 and the curtain referred to in Koran 33: 53, which was meant to separate the man from the woman. This combination of veil and curtain, through a long, slow period of reverse evolution in fundamentalist Muslim societies, could not have produced a more loathsome and sense-less outer garment. Through this special dress, half the population of the Muslim world is deliberately and ma-liciously cut off from the rest of the community.

This segregation does not disturb most Muslim men, as their attitudes are reinforced by almost all of the Muslim theologians, who maintain that the first and most important duty of a woman is toward her husband: to prepare his food, wash his clothes, and satisfy his sexual desires. In other words, she is a loyal and faithful provider of service to her master. Disobeying one's hus-band is a punishable crime in the Koran, as we shall see later. If a man wants to take his wife out to a friend's or relative's house, she most probably cannot refuse, even if she abhors the idea.

In such a gathering, the men sit separately from the women. If they are not in another room, the women's veils are kept on at all times and they are not supposed to be lifted at any time. The women's table is separated and sometimes the men are served before the women. The formality is stiff. Women, if they are permitted to speak, should cast down their eyes and speak in a low tone, as loud laughter or conversation is considered un-ethical. In some orthodox Muslim countries, such as Saudi Arabia, any social gatherings attended by both men and women are considered morally wrong.[7]

When a woman is taken ill, no male physician is al-lowed to examine her except in special cases. A female doctor is usually consulted even though she may not practice the right specialty. In come cases, the man may prefer that his wife or daughter not see a doctor at all.

In many instances, if a male doctor is in attendance,

a sick woman will keep her veil wrapped around herself while her physician examines her. In some communities the doctors feel the woman's pulse through the veil!

There have also been recorded instances in which two lovers have met secretly and had sexual contact without removing the veil from the woman's face. In the eyes of the uneducated fundamentalist girl, revealing her face to a man who is not her next of kin is an unforgivable crime. In fact, it is a capital crime, much more serious than adultery or fornication. Unbelievable as this may sound, it is true.

A Muslim harem is taboo for males. No man is permitted to enter the quarters housing the wives and daughters, and no male except the father and brothers is allowed to see the faces of these girls. After marriage only the husband has this privilege.

In some Islamic universities, especially in the Arab countries of Southwest Asia, women are separated from the male students by a curtain drawn in the classrooms. The female students are not allowed to talk directly to their male instructors, and most of their conversation is carried out from behind a curtain that separates the instructors from the female students.

Arrangements may allow females to use the classrooms on odd days while the male students use them on even days. For example, the university library in Saudi Arabia is allocated to the girls twice a week and no male student is allowed to use the library on those days.

In most Muslim countries, coeducation does not exist at any level of schooling. It is especially rare at the high school level. No mixed sports or recreation is allowed.

According to some schools of thought, women are not allowed to attend the mosques for praying. In other traditions, women may attend the mosques, but they must line up behind the men and boys. This arrangement ensures that the rows of teenaged boys will isolate the women from the men. In the mosque the man cannot see a woman's face, as he is always facing forward toward Mecca.

UNEQUAL TREATMENT OF WOMEN BASED ON THE KORAN

Despite the obvious disparity between men and women in Muslim societies, some Muslim apologists attempt to show that the founder of Islam was very much in favor of equality. They cite one of the hadiths (traditions), according to which Muhammad said: "All people are equal, as equal as the teeth of a comb. There is no claim of merit of an Arab over a non-Arab, or a white over a black person, or a male over a female. Only God-fearing people merit a preference with God."[8] This passage is indeed very egalitarian, and for this very reason it is difficult to attribute such sentiments to Muhammad because they contradict numerous statements in the Koran. The following verses from the Koran prove that this hadith is in complete disagreement with Islam's holy scripture.

1. "And Allah hath favoured some of you above others in provision. Now those who are more favoured will by no means hand over their provision to those (slaves) whom their right hands possess, so that they may be equal with them in respect thereof." (Koran 16: 71)

This verse is clear, explicit, and unequivocal, and it contradicts the above-mentioned hadith completely. According to the Koran, people are not created equal, because Allah has established the special superiority of master over slave. It is clearly indicated that some people have privileges over others in acquiring wealth, and Allah wants it that way.

2. "Allah coineth a similitude: (on the one hand) a (mere) chattel slave, who hath control of nothing, and (on the other hand) one on whom We have bestowed a fair provision from Us, and he spendeth thereof secretly and openly. Are they equal?" (Koran 16: 75)

We notice once again that Allah does not equate a wealthy master with a destitute slave. The last sentence is manifest proof of the inequality, as it asks, "Are they equal?" The answer is of course obvious. The slave does not equal his master.

3. "He [Allah] coineth for you a similitude of yourselves. Have ye, from among those whom your right hands possess [slaves], partners in the wealth We have bestowed upon you, equal with you in respect thereof, so that ye fear them as ye fear each other . . . ?" (Koran 30: 28)

The above verse clearly shows the inequality between master and slave, which was taken for granted in Muhammad's community. Such details about everyday life in the Prophet's day are enough to repudiate the tradition claiming that Muhammad urged all people to be treated equally, like "the teeth of a comb." Islam accepts the institution of slavery and it is evident that any community in which slave-trafficking is practiced cannot treat people equally.

Regarding the inequality between men and women, the Koran states: "Men are superior to women because

Allah has made the one of them to excel over the other and because man provides the subsistence for women." (Koran 4: 34)

What other proof do we need? These are supposedly the words of Allah revealed to his Prophet. Claims for equality of the sexes under Islam contradict its sacred scripture.

MALE SEXUAL INSECURITY AND THE NEED FOR CONTROL

Why is Islam so obsessed with keeping men and women apart? Why have Muslim men gone to such great lengths to maintain control over women? Let us first consider the role of male sexual attitudes dating back to Muhammad, and then we will contrast the status of Muslim women with the role of women in pre-Islamic and ancient Near Eastern cultures.

The Veil as a Check on Male Sexual Desire

The following quote is attributed to Muhammad by a number of hadith collectors: "A woman is a pudendum [awrat] which is proper to hide and cover; therefore when a woman goes out Satan looks at her and desires to carry her from the road."[9] In the eyes of Muhammad, according to this quote, all male believers are potential "Satans" who might try to take unconcealed women for themselves. When this statement was made, most of the residents of Medina were Muhammad's followers, and most of the nonbelievers had been either driven out of the town (like the tribe of Banu Nadir) or butchered (like the Banu Qurayza). Therefore, "Satan" can refer to none other than the Muslim occupants of the town.

It should also be noted that Muhammad himself was one of the men who were unable to control their lust upon looking at women. Recall that he visited the home of Zayd, his adopted son, and there saw Zaynab, Zayd's wife, half-naked. Muhammad's obvious desire for the woman eventually led to the divorce of Zayd from his wife, and shortly thereafter Muhammad married her himself.

It is related by a great number of chroniclers that in the early days of Islam both free and slave women appeared unveiled in the streets, and there was no way to distinguish between the two classes. Therefore, the ordinance of the veil was revealed because in this way the free woman, who was veiled, could be recognized and no one would bother her.[10] This will be discussed in more detail later, when Muhammad's law is compared with that of the ancient world.

The law of the veil is not only humiliating to women, but it is an insult to men. It is a clear indication that, in the eyes of Muhammad, all Muslim males were sex-crazed. The obvious implication is that seeing a woman without a veil would cause the typical Muslim male to lose all control and that unveiled women would constantly be subjected to unwanted sexual advances. One would think that Islam does not trust its own followers to adhere to its teachings of piety, submission to Allah, abstinence, and kindness. Despite all the good deeds that a Muslim male is commanded to do, he is not to be trusted to see an unveiled woman. "Women should not shake hands with men and vice-versa, as that practice is psychologically unsound."[11]

A faith that is so unstable as to be threatened by a handshake between a man and woman is totally out of touch with reality. Maybe the Arabs of the early Islamic period were uncontrollable and Muhammad, out of jealousy or some other personal reason, did not trust them. The contemporary Muslim men who travel to or study in Western countries today and see and meet thousands of young, sometimes beautiful, unveiled non-Muslim women do not seem to be disturbed or out of control. They shake hands, talk, dance, play, and interact with members of the opposite sex without any unseemly conduct. Their own intellect guides them to adapt to the laws of the host countries and to respect the women there.

It is immature to believe that the veil is capable of preventing men from developing sexual desires. The method of protecting the fruits of the orchard from theft or intruders is not to raise a thick, high, impenetrable wall around the garden. The wise and proper way is to declare the owner's rights to his property, apprehend trespassers, and punish law-breakers. To force women to wear the veil is to punish the innocent majority because of a few unstable individuals who might be tempted to commit sexual crimes by the sight of the female form.

This mistaken, ineffective practice of hiding what is desirable is dictated by the Koran:

> And tell the believing women to lower their gaze and be modest [literally, "guard their sex organs"] and to display of their adornment only that which is apparent. (Koran 24: 31)

According to this unequivocal command, the woman is instructed by Allah to cast down her eyes and never look directly at a man, lest he be moved by passion and develop a desire to possess her. In fact, Muhammad was obviously not convinced of the effectiveness of his teachings: in spite of all his pious preaching and the promise of heavenly rewards for Muslims who are clean in their attitudes toward others, he still believed that a glance at a woman's face or her uncovered hair might destroy a man's faith, shattering his will to submit to Allah.

In order to further protect his male faithful from the conflagration of desire caused by a woman's appearance, Muhammad commanded men also to lower their gaze and not to look at women, though they be shrouded from head to foot: "Tell the believing men to lower their gaze and be modest [literally, 'guard their sex organs']." (Koran 24: 30)

This admonition to the faithful to guard their sex organs resulted from ancient styles of clothing. Apparently, the nomadic, pre-Islamic Arabs, unlike the people of the civilized empires such as the Babylonians, Assyrians, Persians, and Egyptians, did not have any use for underwear—the climate was too warm for such garments to be practical. Instead, they wore long linen shirts, a head cover to protect them from the intense heat of the desert sun, and a sandallike shoe made from goat skin. The primitive Arab male and female did not know about trousers, much less underwear. It was not until after the conversion to Islam and the subsequent invasion of Iran that Arabs were introduced to the practice of wearing trousers, which they subsequently adopted.

As they did not wear any kind of trousers, when they

moved about—to mount a camel, for instance—their genitals were sometimes exposed. This was probably one of the reasons that Muhammad had ordered his followers, male and female, to keep covered and to "guard their sex organs." (The Arabic word in the above verses is *furuje*, meaning genitals.)

Not only does the Koran specify that a woman may not look at men other than her blood relatives, but it also does not permit her even to talk with a strange man in a soft, charming voice, since this might stir his passions: "O ye wives of the Prophet! Ye are not like any other woman. If ye keep your duty (to Allah), then be not soft of speech, lest he in whose heart is a disease aspire (to you), but utter customary speech." (Koran 33: 32)

Many jurisprudents, based on the above verse, maintain that even if a woman is talking from behind a curtain or closed door, she must twist her tonality in such a manner so as not to reveal her age or looks to the listener. She is not to converse in the usual soft female voice, lest the man get excited and develop a desire for her.

The prevailing opinion among orthodox Muslim men seems to be that men and women are like fire and gunpowder: in close proximity they're liable to explode from unchecked sexual desire. They should therefore be kept as far apart as possible (through both veiling and seclusion) to reduce the potential for social evils. They criticize Western societies for having prostitution and sexual anarchy, which they believe results from the interaction of the sexes.

This reasoning is certainly without any foundation. Men and women have lived together from the age of primitive tribal communes through the Middle Ages up to the present day. No explosion ever occurred in ancient Egypt, Iran, or China in the past when women lived natural lives unsequestered from men. One cannot say that social evils in countries like France, Germany, and England, where the women are not veiled and kept apart from men, are more rampant than in Pakistan and Bangladesh. Certainly no evil is going to spring up if the Muslim female is freed from the captivity of rigorous religious laws.

As long as the equality of men and women is supported by law, no harm will result from the proximity of male and female. As soon as the supremacy of one sex over the other is perpetuated by the religious laws, however, and the female is driven out of society, screened behind the walls, and subjugated to the male, then the follies and evils begin to show themselves.

The Veil and Marriage

Since legal puberty for a Muslim female, according to the tradition, is attained when she is nine years old, marriage at this age is not uncommon. It is at the age of puberty that females must observe the rule of purdah and cover themselves in some sort of overgarment or veil. "For Muslim women Purdah in the sense of complete veiling seems to operate after puberty in relation to all men except very close kin."[12] Since girls are forced to veil themselves when they are still children, a prospective bridegroom usually cannot see or even talk to his future wife before the marriage. Marriage in such communities is performed with the help of a female broker, usually an elderly woman who is approached by the man or his parents. The prospective groom explains to her what physical characteristics his future wife should have and what his feminine ideals are.

The broker, after hearing the description of the prospective bride, starts to look for a girl with such qualities, which she can usually find within a few days. The broker gives an appealing description of the girl to entice the future husband, and the marriage contract is initiated. All too often, however, on the wedding night, after all of the marriage ceremonies are complete and the girl is handed over to her husband in the bedroom, he finds out, much to his amazement, that she is completely the opposite of what he had requested. Such a blind marriage is all too common in Islamic communities and sometimes ends up in a quick divorce before the marriage is consummated.

Prior to the wedding, the girl is as eager to find out about her future husband. The parents of the boy who initiate the blind marriage naturally lead the girl to believe that he is the best possible choice for her and not infrequently she is lured into accepting a man who is altogether unfit. Either he is much older than his description or he has none of the fine qualities that were detailed by his parents. For example, three of the women who married Muhammad were so ill at ease after entering his bedroom (see chapter 1) that they declared, "I take refuge in Allah," a way of nullifying the marriage agreement, and he was obliged to divorce them the very same evening.

The fate of some girls in blind marriages is much worse than that of those three brides, however. Some women find that their husbands are as old as their grandfathers, and if they cannot get a divorce—which in most cases is not possible because they have no right to divorce—they are bound to live a miserable life.

THE STATUS OF WOMAN IN THE PRE-ISLAMIC PERIOD

Arab Women Enjoyed Greater Freedom Before Muhammad

As has been previously mentioned, the inequality of the sexes was not always the standard in Arabia. Among the early desert dwellers of North Arabia and the bedouin before the time of Muhammad, women wore a simple head covering, which was wrapped around the head and tied at the back of the neck. Complete concealment as it is practiced today did not exist. Arab women were their mates' partners in peace and war, and they accompanied men everywhere. "In ancient Arabia we find many proofs that women moved freely and asserted themselves more strongly than the modern cast."[13]

In short, "The use of the veil was almost unknown in Arabia before Islam nor did the harem system prevail in the days of idolatry."[14] Since most Arabs of this time were "nomads of the desert dwelling in tents,"[15] it would have been impractical for the women to live in concealment. It would have been impossible for them to carry a major share of the day's activities in the midst of the desert if their whole bodies had been wrapped in a cloak. Working-class women, who brought water from distant springs, prepared flour for bread, and were busy with numerous household tasks in and around their simple mud dwellings, did not use a veil other than a simple head covering to protect them from the intense heat. "The veil and seclusion were, by these, unknown and unneeded."[16]

The position of pre-Islamic women was comparatively high and they certainly were not regarded as slaves or chattel, but as equal partners.[17] Among the women of ancient Arabia one could find poets, judges, and business partners. They took part in tribal disputes and in some instances, they were as active as their men in the battles against their adversaries. By reciting lyric poems and beating on tambourines, they encouraged their brothers, husbands, and sons to fight and persevere in battle. Even in the early days of Islam, whenever there was a feud between the pagans of Mecca and Muhammad's followers, the pageantry of these women could be seen in the battlefields. For example, in the battle of Uhud, Hant, a Meccan woman who had lost some of her close male relatives in previous skirmishes, is described as going from one side of the battlefield to the other, encouraging the soldiers of Mecca to defeat the Muslims. The wife of Muhammad's most powerful adversary, one of the Quraysh chieftains of Mecca, she promised to free her strong African slave if he disposed of Hamza, Muhammad's fearless and youngest uncle. He did so and thus earned his freedom.

Women at that time were really free and enjoyed a better life than was later offered by Islam. They were the assets of the tribes because they were the mothers of future generations, as well as a source of income. Therefore, by bringing more women to the tribe, either as captives or otherwise, men were able to increase their numbers, thus adding to the physical strength of the tribe. In fact, each woman was treated as the mother of a future swordsman. In terms of their economic worth, recall that a bride-price was paid when a marriage was contracted. Thus, fathers welcomed newborn daughters as a potential source of wealth. Even when a father gave his daughter away for a specified bride-price, two conditions or unwritten rules were usually observed. First, the marriage had to be made on the basis of an equal match and second, the bride was not to be sent away against her consent. For these reasons, tribes would raid each other with the objective of capturing as many women as possible. Thus, women were considered the most valuable possession and were carefully guarded.[18] We have already noted that Muhammad raided neighboring tribes in the early days of Islam to capture as many women and children as he could. In this aim he was instinctly following the customs of his forefathers.

Pre-Islamic women also enjoyed far more sexual freedom than Muslim women today. At times they even "entertained" their husbands' friends:

> A panorama of female sexual rights in pre-Islamic culture reveals that women's sexuality was not bound by the concept of legitimacy. Children belonged to the mother's clan. Women had sexual freedom to enter into and break unions with more than one man.[19]

Naturally, in the context of such matrimonial rites, some of which may be considered too liberal even by today's standards in industrialized societies, there was no place for the veil.

Archeological evidence also indicates the relatively high status of Arab women before Islam. Zwemer says, "According to Nöldeke and Grimme, the Nabathian and South Arabian coins and inscriptions prove that women held an independent and honorable position."[20]

Pre-Islamic Arab women had the right to choose their mates and to divorce them whenever they wanted to. Muhammad's first wife, Khadija, is a good example of the freedom of the woman to find her own man. She was the one who offered her hand and proposed marriage, through a middleman, to Muhammad, who accepted immediately because of her wealth and prestige.

Khadija, however, may have been among the last group of Arab women to have such freedom. In fact, the advent of Islam and the introduction of Allah's divine law has certainly worked against women's freedom and driven them out of society's activities. The veil, the curtain, and seclusion ordained by Allah in the Koran have caused the position of woman to deteriorate. "The place of the woman," writes Smith, "in the family and in the society, has strictly declined under his [Muhammad's] law."[21]

Female Infanticide in Pre-Islamic Arabia:
Exaggerated Muslim Accounts

Despite the evidence that women had more rights in pre-Islamic Arabia than they do under Islam, many Muslim apologists insist that the lot of women was improved by Muhammad. To back up this claim they refer to the cruel custom of female infanticide, which had been practiced in pagan Arabia. They point to Koran 60: 12, which describes an oath of allegiance that fugitive women from idolatrous tribes had to take to Muhammad: among other things they were enjoined not to kill their children. Muslim clerics and commentators on the Koran take great pride in this ordinance. They credit Muhammad with stopping a savage rite.

Many Muslim writers relate very sad stories about this practice. Hundreds of accounts are related in which the father of the female child, after burying the child alive, would regret the act. 'Uthman, one of Muhammad's sons-in-law and the third caliph, is reported to have said that he could never forget the sight of his daughter's burial, because when he put her in the ditch and started to cover her with sand, she reached up and touched his face with her hand to brush off some particles of sand in his beard.

Stories such as this are enough to move anyone in favor of a man who is said to have stopped such cruelty. However, contrary to what Islamic writers claim about female infanticide in pre-Islamic Arabia, there is reason to believe that the practice was not common at all.

First, based on the number of women in pre-Islamic Arabia, it does not appear that the female population was intentionally curtailed in any way. In fact, at times there seem to have been more women than men. As noted in chapter 3, one of the reasons given by Muslim apologists in favor of polygamy was that there were far more women that men. This would indeed be paradoxical if female infants were frequently killed by their fathers.

Furthermore, in a society where women are regarded as valuable booty in tribal raids, a father would have no motive for killing his daughters. If men raided other tribes to acquire more women than they naturally had, it stands to reason that women were highly valued. Daughters were a source of income for the family since each one represented a certain bride-price for future bridegrooms. Some historians have suggested that in some cases in which the men were not capable of defending the tribe against more powerful marauders, they would kill their young daughters rather than face the disgrace of seeing them abducted.[22] This may have occasionally happened, but was certainly not the norm.

Finally, what we know of pre-Islamic poetry indicates that women were frequently celebrated, along with wine and camels, as a source of pleasure and pride. In addition, as noted above, pre-Islamic women had more rights than women under Islam. In such a context, it seems unlikely that female infanticide would have been sanctioned.

In every society, of course, there are parents who cannot afford to have more children, and in desperate situations caused by famine or drought, such impoverished people might resort to infanticide. But this was a rare event and certainly not the standard of behavior. A verse in the Koran (6: 152) makes it clear that when infanticide did occur, it was caused by poverty: "Slay not your children, fearing a fall to poverty. We shall provide for them and for you. Lo! the slaying of them is a great sin."

Perhaps the notion of widespread female infanticide in pre-Islamic Arabia came from the well-known story of Qays, chief of the Temim tribe. He was defeated in battle and his daughter was captured by Nu'man, the prince of Hirrah. Later the girl fell in love with her captor and refused to go back to her father, even though he was eager to ransom her. It is said that the father in anger swore an oath that he would kill any future daughters that he might have and subsequently buried ten female infants.[23]

Even if this story could be proved true, it was one case only and does not imply the widespread practice of infanticide. It seems that Muhammad has been credited with abolishing a savage custom that at its worst was a rare phenomenon.

The Veil in the Pre-Islamic Period

Some chroniclers attribute the order of the veil to 'Umar, Muhammad's father-in-law and close friend. It is written that 'Umar told Muhammad it is proper to order his wives to wear veils because some men who enter his house may have wicked minds. Another story relates "that one day Muhammad was seated with Aisha when a passerby Arab admiring her beauty offered Muhammad a camel for her and this produced the order for veiling."[24] But even if these stories are true, the custom of wearing a veil for one reason or another dates back to the ancient Near East, many centuries before the time of Muhammad.

Fakiki, one of the authorities in Islamic history, states that in the pre-Islamic period a type of head covering was worn by married Arab women to distinguish them from eligible single women in public places like the Ka'aba, the Okaz (a commodities market), or at the annual fair held between the cities of Taif and Nakhlah.[25] In such public gathering places, suitors would seek young women as prospective brides. In those days the veil was simply a large scarf which the woman wore over her head and shoulders. A broad band of fabric was worn loosely over the head, about the neck, and sometimes around the waist. The face and hands of the woman remained uncovered. Thus, the veil was originally more a garment of class distinction, intended as a means of distinguishing married women from unmarried girls. Only free women wore the veil; slaves were not required to and in most cases were not allowed to.

This insignia separating married from unmarried women and free women from slaves did not originate in Arabia. The custom can be traced back to ancient Assyria. In the Middle Assyrian Law, promulgated in the fifteenth century B.C.E., we find ordinances pertaining to the wearing of the veil. Law 40 of this Assyrian code stipulates that every free woman must wear a veil:

> If the wives of a man, or the daughters of a man or his women go out into the street, their heads [are to be veiled]. . . . [As for widows] their heads . . . are to be veiled.
>
> When [they go out] into the streets . . . they shall veil themselves. The concubines (captured women) who go to the streets apart from their mistress are to be veiled.
>
> The (sacred) prostitute, whom a husband has married, is to be veiled in the streets. But one whom a husband has not married is to have her head uncovered in the streets. She is not to veil herself; her head is to be uncovered.
>
> The one who sees a veiled harlot is to seize her, se-

cure witnesses, (and) bring her for the judgment of the palace. . . . Fifty blows they shall inflict upon her. Bitumen they shall pour on her head. . . .

Maid servants (hand-maids) are not to veil themselves.[26]

The following similarities between this ancient law and ordinances in the Koran are noteworthy:

1. In Assyrian law wives and their daughters are instructed to cover their heads when they leave the house. Koran 33: 59 has a nearly identical instruction: "O Prophet! Tell thy wives and thy daughters and the women of the believers to draw their cloaks close round them (when they go out). That will be better so that they may be recognized and not bothered."

2. In Assyrian law, the concubines of a man who go out into the streets must have a veil; according to Islam, all the concubines of a man are to veil themselves outside of their homes.

3. In Assyrian law, if a man married a prostitute, she must behave like a chaste woman by veiling herself; in Islamic law, when a man marries a harlot, she is to repent from her past and veil herself.

4. In Assyrian law, prostitutes are not to veil themselves; according to the jurisprudence of Islam, an unveiled woman is regarded as a prostitute.

5. Assyrian law enjoins that any prostitute who veils herself will receive fifty blows and pitch shall be poured on their head; according to most Islamic exegetes, if a woman does not veil herself properly she will be flogged and her hair shorn.

6. In Assyrian law captive women or slave girls are not permitted to be veiled; in Islamic jurisprudence veiling of captive women is not ordained.

7. Assyrian law designates the veil as the visible sign distinguishing a married woman or noble girl from a prostitute. Thus, men on the streets would know not to make sexual advances to veiled women. Likewise, the Koran explicitly states that married women and their daughters must wear veils when they go out "so that they may be recognized and not bothered." (Koran 33: 59)

Further comparisons can be drawn regarding the treatment of captive women. Ancient Assyrian law specifies the rules for marrying a captive girl:

> If a man wishes to veil his concubine, he shall have five or six of his neighbors present (and) veil her in their presence (and) say, "She is my wife," (thus) she is his wife. A captive girl who is not veiled in the presence of the men, whose husband did not say, "She is my wife," she is not a wife. She remains a captive woman. If the man dies not having sons by his veiled wife, the sons of the captive woman shall be their sons; they shall receive a portion (of the parental estate).[27]

In Islamic law if a man marries a captive woman, he must do it in the presence of the witnesses and then veil her so that it becomes formal and everyone knows that she is married to him. An example from the life of Muhammad is the taking of his wife Safiyya (the widow of a chieftain whom Muhammad had defeated and killed). The event, as related by al-Bukhari, illustrates some parallels with the Assyrian law:

Anas narrated [as follows]: The prophet stayed for three days between Khaybar and Medina, and there he consummated his marriage to Saffiya. The Muslims wondered, "Is she considered as his wife or slave?" Then they said, "If he orders her to veil herself, she will be one of the mothers of the believers [meaning Muhammad's wives], but if he does not order her to veil herself, she will be a slave-girl." Muhammad threw his own mantle on her in front of everyone, and took her to his own harem.[28]

Assyrian law ordains the veil for the captive girls and prostitutes who get married; Koranic law requires the same thing. Therefore, it is not unreasonable to suggest that Muhammad perpetuated a pagan law under the banner of monotheism. In any case, the very law once practiced by the ancient Assyrians found its way into the Koran and is being applied even today by all Muslims.

ISLAM TODAY: THE ECONOMIC DISADVANTAGES OF INEQUALITY AND THE SECLUSION OF WOMEN

Because of the deep-rooted conviction in the Muslim societies of the Middle East and Africa that women are destined only to bring up children, whereas men are responsible for earning a living and providing for their families, women's employment outside of the home is a rare exception. Some of these Muslim communities are at poverty level and finding employment for men is difficult, if not impossible, so employment for women in these places is out of the question. Yet the irony is that the underdeveloped Muslim countries are disadvantaged due to the fact that half of their population—namely, the women—are merely consumers who are not permitted to produce anything because of religious restrictions. Poverty is a social ill that should be overcome through sustained economic growth. However, economic growth is not possible if the total consumption of goods and services exceeds their total production. It is a vicious cycle: the country is underdeveloped because the Gross National Product (GNP) is low. Therefore, the per capita income is low and personal savings are reduced with the result that the level of investment is low, ending in unemployment. In the absence of full employment, the overall GNP will fall. The capitalist countries, on the advice of their economists, have devised different methods for improving the overall economic outlook of their people, but progress is hindered by religious tenets.

Women, by taking part in the social activities of their communities and by sharing the responsibilities with men in the modern and advanced countries, can contribute to the betterment and welfare of the land they live in, and thus improve the standard of living in their own countries. This fact must be acknowledged and acted upon for true progress to take place.

A few Islamic countries, such as Saudi Arabia, Kuwait, and Iraq, have prospered because of their oil deposits. The sale of oil brings in billions of dollars each year into their economies. Those countries, thanks to the oil needs of the world, have been able to increase their per capita income to such a level that in some cases it exceeds that of the United States, Western Europe, and Japan. But material prosperity is the only similarity between these Islamic nations and their wealthy Western trading partners. Aside from their incredible oil incomes, high standards of living, and modern facilities such as telecommunications, transportation, and factories, these countries suffer from the same social ills as the poor Islamic countries. Despite wealth and grandiose projects, the female half of the population in these lands is deprived of basic freedoms: the freedom to choose a husband; to choose the color of her garments; to move around in society; to pursue a chosen occupation; to initiate a divorce when she is subjected to domestic cruelty; to participate in political activities; to vote and to run for political office.

CONCLUSION

The struggle between the upholders of women's seclusion and the advocates of women's emancipation is not over yet. In fact, it is just beginning to manifest itself. The proponents of seclusion maintain that sexual desire is an uncontrollable phenomenon and both sexes must therefore be kept apart. They believe that a man and woman together are like "a live ember by the side of a mine of gun powder."[29] In the eyes of such people, men and women have no willpower at all and their proximity will end in catastrophe. To them such restraining influences as the civil code, law enforcement, education, self-discipline, morality, and religion, in short, everything that historically has checked unbridled sexual passion, are without effect. These people reject the science of psychology and repudiate the ability of human minds to acquire refined behavior. To them men and women are like beasts in heat who will explode with sexual passion as soon as they see each other. Thus, they must be kept apart.

The defenders of the veil imply that the female sex is by nature inferior. By this way of thinking, creating equality between the sexes would upset the balance of nature and nothing in society could be accomplished.

> If both of them [men and women] are equal in power and no one has dominance or control over the other, neither of them will accept the effect of the other, and no action will then take place at all. If the cloth has the same hardness as the needle, no act of sewing will at all be accomplished. If the earth were so hard and impervious as not to accept the effect of the plough or pickaxe, agriculture or architecture would not be possible.[30]

Thus it is the inequality of man and woman that enables any work to be performed at all. Without this inequality nothing would get done! This apologist and others like him think that human society is composed of two classes, one active, dominant, and strong (the men), and the other passive, submissive, and weak (women). Needless to say, this sort of reasoning is promoted to prove the Koranic law, which regards man as the superior sex. This same author prophesies a perilous future for any society in which the "natural" division of labor is abolished and women perform similar jobs as men. For such communities he foresees destruction: "Any civilization that tries to abolish this division of labor may temporarily achieve some degree of progress or glory, but its ultimate destruction is inevitably certain."[31] No reason is given for this prophecy.

Of course, we don't know what the future might hold for a civilization in which all men and women enjoy equal rights. But it is certain that as long as Islam secludes women from society, no real socio-economic progress is possible. How can a society advance when its influential religious leaders continue to make statements like this: "Nature has given man superiority over woman. For her there is only slavery, and know it well that she cannot be emancipated from his bondage"?[32]

6

WIFE BEATING—
ALLAH'S ORDINANCE

As for those [women] from whom you fear rebellion, admonish them and banish them to the bed apart and scourge them.

—Koran 4: 34

In accordance with the above revelation, when a husband calls his wife to his bed to have sexual intercourse, she must obey without a word no matter what her condition may be. She may be physically sick or simply indignant and indisposed, but that does not change the circumstance at all.

Muhammad is quoted as saying, "If a man invites his wife to sleep with him and she refuses to come to him, then the angels send their curses on her until morning."[1] Thus, the wife of a Muslim should always be ready to come to bed and satisfy her husband's sensual desires; otherwise, she may be beaten by him and cursed by the angels of Allah, who apparently are commissioned to have a close watch over sexual affairs of a couple.

It is important to note that the word *rebellion* as used in the above quotation refers to any disobedience on the part of the female mate, not simply reluctance to engage in sex. If she refuses to sleep with her husband or does not obey his command, she will be admonished first, and later, the man is permitted by Allah to scourge his wife. The apologists hold that when the wife rebels against her mate, and her rebellion is of the "ordinary" nature, then she is admonished only.[2] M. 'Ali says:

> It appears that confining [women] to the house is the first step, and it is when they repeat their evil deeds in the house, or do not submit to the authority of the husband and desert him, that permission is given to inflict corporal punishment, which is the last resort, and even if this step does not make them mend their ways, matrimonial relations may be ended.[3]

In other words, if a woman merely resists her husband's wish or his authority, the Koran provides advice on how to handle her. If she hates her husband and resists his sensual desires, "a stronger remedy is suggested," and the husband is allowed to separate his bed or manifest his disapproval by separating himself from her while living in the same house as man and wife. Any disobedience and further misconduct of the wife beyond this degree necessitates scourging or beating followed by repudiation.

Islamic jurisprudence, moreover, allows a husband to withhold the maintenance of a rebellious wife. A wife who refuses to go to bed and sleep with her man whenever he feels like it and requires her to do so is not entitled to subsistence, or even clothing or lodging. Muslim law grants the husband whose wife refuses sexual intercourse "the right to withhold maintenance from her (food, clothing, and lodging) which is normally his duty to provide."[4] The Muslim wife must be totally under the authority of her husband. She must be submissive to him and must carry out all of his commands except those which make her deny her faith. This belief is so fundamental to Islamic culture that even some educated Muslim women support it. For example, one such woman has written the following:

Man is such that he considers a good wife as the one who gives no opportunity for reproach. . . . She never criticizes or finds fault with her husband's whims and fancies. She places implicit faith in him and bows to her tin-god. In short, her duty is to obey unquestioningly and yield to her lord every moment of her life.[5]

Another Islamic writer maintains:

As far as possible, keep the heart of your husband in your hand, and obey his slightest wish. Should he bid you stand with folded hands in his presence all through the night, then know that your welfare in this life and the next depends on your doing so. . . . Never do anything to vex him. Even if he should call the daytime "night," you must acquiesce.[6]

Thus, blind obedience on the part of the married woman is expected by the Muslim jurisprudents.

As the quote that opened this chapter shows, the "legitimacy" of wife beating derives from the Koran, which has dictated the supremacy of men over women. The clergy, especially the exegetes and interpreters of the scripture, hold that this superiority is due to man's higher mental ability and good counsel. "Therefore, if a man should do less than his duty to his wife, she should not be unmindful of his essential superiority."[7]

Despite claims such as this, the Muslim apologists try to justify the Koranic ordinance by which a husband may beat his wife if he deems it necessary:

> It cannot be denied that cases do happen when this extreme step [wife beating] becomes necessary, but these are exceptional cases and their occurrence is generally limited to the rougher strata of society where the remedy of slight corporal punishment is not only unobjectional but necessary.[8]

This is far from the truth, however. Wife beating is not an exceptional case, but rather it is common practice among the poor classes in Muslim communities. Although some may say that the beating and scourging of wives by their husbands is limited to "the rougher strata of society," unfortunately, many Muslim societies, especially those in Asia and Africa, are poor. Therefore, "the rougher strata" comprises the whole, or at least the majority, of the people.

The corporal punishment ordained by Allah in the Koran is interpreted in many different ways. Some say that it means only a light beating with the hands, such as slapping or striking with the fist. Others argue that the woman should be flogged with a whip or rod, while still other jurists maintain that the beating must be implemented in such a way that no sign of maltreatment is left on her body. The methods of beating also vary among the different geographical regions: "Wife beating is allowed by the Koran, and the method and limitations are explained by the laws of the religion."[9] Slapping, kicking, beating with fists, scourging, flogging, and hitting with sticks or rods are all mentioned in Islamic books. Each man, according to his conscience, education, culture, background, and family ties may treat his disobedient wife as he sees fit.[10] No matter what the degree or method of punishment, however, all seem to agree that a rebellious woman, one who does not submit to the sexual desires of her husband whenever he calls her to bed, must be beaten.

The law of wife-beating is a one-way street. A man may strike his wife, but the woman may not do the same. A woman is not allowed to beat her mate even if she is able to defend herself by striking back. If she does, she will be sent to jail.[11] A man may ask the Islamic judge to compel his wife to surrender to his sexual desires, but the woman cannot accuse her husband of maltreatment. If she tried, the court would reject her claim. A woman cannot file suit against her husband for beating her; no Islamic court would convene for such a claim. The man may continue the physical punishment as long as his wife does not surrender to his sexual desires. In the Arab communities, the institution is called *ta'a*, which means the submission of a wife to her husband's will and desire no matter what her opinion of him. She must submit to his caprices even if he is brutal in his approach to her. She may not leave the conjugal roof. Her feelings toward her mate carry no weight at all and he can keep her in his possession against her consent.

In fact, the absolute power of the husband to correct his wife when she is rebellious to him is of such magnitude that even the Indian government was obliged to recognize the Koranic law of wife beating. We quote from Wilson:

> This marital power of correction (recognized by the Mohammedan law) has never been expressly taken away by the Indian legislature, and wife beating confined to "moderate chastisement" may be taken out of the criminal law of the land provided that there is absence of "actual violence" of such a character as to endanger personal health or safety.[12]

Thus, the Indian legislature implicitly accepts the Koranic law for the correction of the wife by her husband. Beating a wife as long as there is no sign of violence on her body is not a criminal act and cannot be prosecuted. There is, however, a distinction made between moderate chastisement and harsh correction. In the first case, the man who beats his wife moderately without leaving a sign on her body cannot be brought to court on the grounds of cruelty. If, however, the chastisement is practiced in such a way to reveal the marks of violence, the law will step in.

Evidence implies that many hundreds of thousands of Indian Muslim women throughout history have been mistreated, but no sign of their complaints can be found in the courts. In fact, there is no place for these oppressed women to turn in a complaint. The Koran gives men the authority to correct their wives whenever they think it proper, and women must submit, as civil law, too, sides with the man and accepts no complaints of the oppressed wife unless the violence is of such character as to endanger her safety. If she is slapped repeatedly, but shows no mark of violence on her body such as would threaten her health, no court, religious or otherwise, will accept her complaint or suit.

As has been pointed out, the words and deeds of the founder of Islam are as important in Muslim jurisdiction as the Koranic law. It is reported that Muhammad said: "And be careful of your duty to Allah in the matter of the women, for you have taken them as the trust of Allah . . . and they owe to you this obligation that they will not allow any one to come into your house when you do not like. If they do, then give them slight corporal punishment which may not leave any effect on their bodies."[13] According to this, wife beating is enjoined by Muhammad's scripture and also affirmed by him personally. This tradition (hadith) contradicts those apologists who try to deny that Allah permitted the striking of wives. Once Muhammad even compared the beating of a wife with that of a slave and stated that corporal punishment of a wife should not be as harsh as that of a bond-woman (a slave). In fact, the Muslim apologists tell us that "great stress is laid on the kind of treatment of women."[14] It is true that in some verses of the Koran the believers are advised to treat women with kindness, but it is also a fact that passages in the Koran are often contradictory.

The adaptation of this "divine law" all depends on who is interpreting the verses and for what reasons. A few examples follow to emphasize this point.

In the Koran it is stated: "There is no coercion in religion" (Koran 2: 256) and: "Unto you your religion, and unto me my religion." (Koran 109: 6) These verses can be cited as proof that Islam is very liberal in its religious thought. According to these verses, no one should be forced to accept Islam, and everyone is free to have his own religion. The Muslim and non-Muslim are both free to practice their own beliefs according to their religion.

However, in the very same Koran, we read: "Kill such of those who have been given Scripture [the Jews and the Christians] as believe not in Allah nor the Last Day. . . . Follow not the religion of truth [Judaism or Christianity] until they pay the tribute readily, being brought low." (Koran 9: 29) Thus, a Muslim is instructed to fight against followers of other religions and kill them if they do not accept Islam or do not pay tribute. In fact, the mode of payment itself is indeed humiliating. The Muslim tax collector draws his sword and holds it over the head of the non-Muslim handing over the tribute (money). This is what the Koran means by the phrase "being brought low."

In two other passages, Muhammad instructs his followers to kill the disbelievers: "O Ye who believe! Kill those of the disbelievers who are near to you and let them find harshness in you" (Koran 9: 123) and "Slay them [non-believers] wherever you find them." (2: 191) The divine law that decrees "unto you your religion, and unto me my religion" now orders its followers to fight and kill every disbeliever who is near them, even if they happen to be close relatives. These passages are sufficient to prove the inconsistencies of Muhammad's book.

The status of and behavior toward women are treated equally erratically, and these inconsistencies may be attributed to the fact that in the early days of the revelation, when he was weak and without substantial support, Muhammad admonished constraint and kindness (perhaps in an attempt to convert his listeners). But as soon as he gained power and the number of his followers began to increase, Muhammad changed his attitudes toward the nonbelievers and women, and ordered harsh treatment. Despite the attempts of some apologists to emphasize that the Koran stresses "the kind treatment of women," the fact remains that the founder of Islam promoted and promulgated the barbaric law of wife beating.

Muslim males, from the early days of Islam up to modern times, have practiced wife beating whenever they wished. The illiterate and uneducated Muslim male "knows" that man is superior to woman because the verses of the Koran explicitly say so. They are also aware of the fact that the apostle of Allah has permitted them, in the holy scripture, to beat their wives if they deny their husbands' wishes. The explanations of the apologists claiming otherwise are nonsensical in the light of the reality of this common practice.

In spite of all the apologistic interpretations and cover-ups, the indisputable fact is that men and women do not enjoy equal rights under Islam. The man, according to the text of the Koran and the words of Muhammad, is superior to woman; he is granted the right to beat his wife if he thinks that is the proper way to bring her back to her senses; she must be obedient to him in every aspect of their mutual life; she cannot leave his house without permission; and last, but not least, he has absolute power for divorce (this will be the topic of the next chapter).

This inequality is further demonstrated by the fact that no limitations are placed on the Muslim male in regard to the beating or flogging of a wife. It is true that some of the apologists would like to justify the law by claiming that physical punishment must be very light, but in communities where the Koranic law (Shariah) rules, women have no right to complain, and there is no limit to the act of beating. It is simply the husband, who may not be bound by any deep humanitarian conviction, who decides when and where he must stop the cruel act. In this sense, Muslim jurisprudence sometimes sounds like the Middle Assyrian Law, which enjoins: "Apart from the punishment specified in the law for married woman, a husband could scourge his wife, pluck her hair, twist or pierce ears, with no liability attaching to him."[15]

The similarity between this law, promulgated during the reign of Tiglath-Pileser, an autocratic polytheist of the ancient world, and the Koranic law of Allah's Prophet is striking. Once more we notice that the law made by Muhammad in the seventh century C.E. is almost identical to an Assyrian law dating some fifteen centuries before our era. It is not illogical and imprudent, therefore, to deduce that wife beating is a remnant of an old custom of a barbaric age, when the wife was treated as the property of the husband. The custom survived in the form of a manmade law in Assyria and was passed on as a

nomadic tradition from generation to generation until
Muhammad universalized it as the command of Allah.

Let us review what Babylonia of the seventeenth century B.C.E. had to offer in regard to a woman who hated
her husband and would not submit to his sexual desires:

> If a woman so hated her husband that she has de-
> clared, "You may not have me," her record shall be in-
> vestigated at the city council and, if she was careful
> (kept herself chaste) and was not at fault, even though
> her husband has been going out and disparaging her
> greatly, that woman, without incurring any blame at
> all, may take her dowry and go off to her father's
> house.[16]

Even a liberal-minded Muslim will agree that this
law of ancient Babylonia is far more progressive than the
cruel and prejudiced law of Muhammad.

Beating a human being is a savage act, and beating a
woman is sheer barbarism. There is nothing more
humiliating for a woman than to be beaten by her mate.
The Koranic law here, like almost all of its ordinances
regarding the woman, is ungodly and inhuman.

Muhammad demands complete submission of the
woman to her man. He makes her the property of her
husband; gives him the authority to admonish her, separate his bed from her, subject her to corporal punishment; and, if she still refuses to comply with his forceful
desires, to repudiate her with one or two words. A
woman who hates her husband and does not surrender
to his sexual desires and passions must be punished by
Allah's command.

From the time of Muhammad up to the present many millions of Muslim males have exposed their wives to harsh treatment and beating. In many cases terrible blows have resulted in death, miscarriage, broken bones, or other injury, such as losing an eye or ear or becoming permanently crippled.

The perpetrators of these deeds believe corporal punishment is necessary to bring women back to their senses. It is regrettable, if not astonishing, that there are still some people in the twentieth century who view women in the same primitive way the desert wanderers of Arabia thirteen hundred years ago did.

7

REPUDIATION OF A WIFE: MALE ABSOLUTE POWER

In the old days, the desert Arab wanderers used to tie their camels' legs and shackle them with a rope or a strap so that the beasts would be unable to walk away from the tent or camp. In a pasture, the camels would be untethered and allowed to graze on the grass. To release a camel from a tether was called *talaq*, and this term has come to mean to release a wife from the marriage bond, in other words, divorce. The expression appears in both the Koran and Muslim law books.

In most parts of the Arab world, the camel has been replaced by expensive luxury cars, but the repudiation of a wife is still as simple and easy as the untethering of a camel! According to the Koran and Islamic law, a man has the right to terminate his marriage whenever and wherever he pleases. It is the absolute power of a Muslim male to repudiate his wife unilaterally at his discretion. He needs no reason for a divorce; a family quarrel or bad temper is sufficient.[1] Divorce does not require any court, judge, lawyer, or counselor. One phrase from a husband is enough to break the marriage bond: "you are divorced."

The Koran states: "If ye wish to exchange one wife for another . . ." (4: 20), giving the absolute power to the man to repudiate his wife and marry another without any formalities.[2] In fact, more than two dozen verses in Allah's scripture explain the modes of divorce (Koran 2: 226, 227, 228, 230–37, 241, 242; 4: 19–21, 130; 33: 49; 58: 3, 4; 63: 1–7; 4: 35).

According to Islamic law, when a man wishes to divorce his wife, all he has to do is to say: "You are divorced," or "You are dismissed," and the wife is thrown out of the house. Sometimes merely pointing his finger at the door is enough to dismiss his wife for good. Phrases like "Join your folk!" or "Your affairs are in your own hand" indicate to the wife that she has been repudiated. The husband can even express his intention by simply dropping three pebbles without further elaboration. Jones writes, "A mere word of divorce uttered by him is enough to render her homeless and throw her, along with children that he has given her, on the public street to beg, borrow or steal."[3]

The woman released from marriage by her husband may not remarry for at least three months; she must observe a waiting period of three menstrual cycles. "O prophet! When you divorce the woman, divorce them for their prescribed or waiting period." (Koran 65: 1) During this waiting period, which is called *idda*, the husband can revoke the divorce as easily as he performed it, simply by calling his wife back to live with him as his lawful mate. No marriage ceremony for this reunification is required. Just as the divorce occurred without any witness or legal steps, so may the husband call his wife back during her three-month waiting period, also without any need for legal procedure. The husband may go to the woman, hold her hand and bring her back to his house, or merely call her back via an arbiter or telephone. By returning to her former husband, the woman acquires the status of a wife once more. Divorce in such cases is called revocable, whereas after the expiration of three months, the divorce is irrevocable.

A man may divorce a wife and call her back up to three times. After the third repudiation, he cannot take her back again unless she marries and is separated from someone else first. The second husband is called *mohallel*, a legalizer, or someone whose act will make it possible for the first husband to bring back his former wife. The Koran is very explicit about this kind of go-between reunification: "And if he hath divorced her (the third time), then she is not lawful unto him thereafter until she hath wedded another husband. Then if he (the other husband) divorce her, it is no sin for both of them that they come together again, if they consider that they are able to observe the limits of Allah." (Koran 2: 230)

This is a rather strange law and is most likely based on the barbaric Arab rite in which the man would send his wife to sleep with someone else for pleasure, money, or to conceive a child by the other man (see chapter 2). By requiring a second husband, Muhammad legalized and perpetuated this pre-Islamic custom.

The ordinance of Allah is very clear: "She is not

lawful unto him thereafter until she hath wedded another husband." In other words, a man is not allowed to take his wife back into his home unless some other man sleeps with her and then releases her first. The second marriage must be genuine and the consummation must be real. No fake marriage or subterfuge wedding is acceptable to Islamic law. This ordinance of Allah proves once more that Islam, like many cults, treats the woman as the property of man. Although a husband repudiates his wife, he has more right to her than anyone else, but after the third pronouncement, he forfeits this right.[4]

When the husband and wife both agree to separate peacefully and the aversion is mutual, it is called *mubarat*, or mutual consent. Divorce by mutual consent, astonishing as it seems, is practiced in Islam, but it is an exception rather than the rule.

A woman can sue for divorce in the Islamic court on specific grounds, such as the impotency of her husband, nonpayment of maintenance, or his insanity. Recall from chapter 6 that cruelty, however, is not sufficient grounds for divorce because wife beating is enjoined in the Koran. When a woman applies to the court for an injunction of divorce, and the husband is not willing to repudiate her, the procedure can be very lengthy and in most cases is futile.

A woman, therefore, cannot repudiate her spouse as easily as a man, unless her right to do so is clearly specified in the marriage contract and a clause is incorporated therein to empower her to file for a divorce. Sometimes the wife who is desperate to be freed from marriage agrees to pay a specified amount of money to her husband for her release.

The offering of financial consideration of some sort is commonly the repayment of the bride-price. As was detailed in chapter 2, when the marriage is contracted, a sum of money is stipulated to be paid by the husband to the wife or her male kinsmen before or after the wedding. This is called *mahr* (bride-price), which means marriage settlement or dowry. A man who divorces his wife must pay the full amount of the specified bride-price except in special cases in which only one-half of the amount is paid. For example, a man can divorce his wife before he consummates his marriage. In such cases, the wife is entitled to half of the dowry or bride price. "If ye divorce them before ye have touched them and ye have appointed unto them a portion, then (pay the) half of that which ye appointed, unless they (the women) agree to forgo it." (Koran 2: 237)

The above so-called revelation is another proof that the dowry is nothing but the bride-price of the woman, as was fully explained earlier. (See chapter 2.)

When the wife agrees to buy her freedom, it is called *khula* in Arabic, which means something belonging to the wife is taken away from her. The bride-price belongs to the wife and is paid to her. When she proposes to give it back to her husband against her freedom, something is taken away from the wife, i.e., her dowry.

Thus, the wife has to forfeit her bed-wage, either the whole or portion of it, and the husband agrees to divorce her for that sum of money. In fact, according to the Koran, Allah is not desirous or willing to release a woman from her marriage bond unless forfeiture of her dowry is rendered: "There is no sin for either of them if the woman ransom herself." (Koran 2: 229) The text of the scripture makes clear that the wife is actually paying money to her husband to get her freedom. This is ransom money, reminiscent of the ancient Arabian nomad's rite, which allowed the release of the booty or captive of the raids after receiving a ransom or head-price.

The ransom money, which a wife pays for her separation from her unmatched husband, may be occasionally higher than the amount of the bride-price. Sometimes, a crooked-minded man marries the daughter of a wealthy family, and then drives her to the point of asking for a divorce through mental and physical oppression. In this case, the parents of the girl would be willing to hand over an exorbitant sum of money for her release.

This kind of repudiation, where the wife secures her freedom by offering financial retribution, although classified as divorce by mutual consent, is plain extortion. The wife agrees to pay the ransom because there is no other way out for her. Otherwise, she is condemned to a painful and torturous life. If the amount of the dowry is inadequate and the woman's folks are not rich enough to meet the demand of the greedy husband, the unhappy life of the wife drags on as long as the man does not give in.

Thus, in Islam a man actually buys his wife when he bargains over the bride-price (*mahr*) and sells his wife's freedom back to her when a financial settlement is paid by her for a divorce. The merit of the bride-price, according to some Islamic jurists, is to make one think twice before asking for a divorce. "The dowry is a check on the party who wants to divorce."[5] Thus, if a husband divorces his wife, he must pay the bride-price; if the wife seeks the divorce, she may forfeit the total amount or some part of her *mahr*. If the bride-price is not specified in the marriage contract and the man divorces his wife, he must pay a sum of money equivalent to the marriage price of any other woman of her social standing. If the marriage is not consummated and the bride-price is not stipulated in the contract, the wife receives something from her prospective husband as a gift whenever he repudiates her and dissolves the marriage. The measure or value of the gratuity depends upon the ability and the wealth of the man. If he is rich, he must give a divorce present to his wife worthy of his capacity and social status, as the Koran enjoins: "Give her a present, the rich according to his wealth and the poor according to his poverty."

As was discussed previously, the bride-price for the woman is usually based on her social status. If she is not from a well-to-do family, her bed-wage would be lower. In most Muslim communities like Sudan, Bangladesh, Pakistan, and India, women do not enjoy a high standard of living. This puts them in a lesser position to buy their release from the husband. Millions of Muslim wives may be willing to ransom themselves but are unable to arrange the financial demand.

"THE ACT MOST HATED BY GOD"

The absolute power of Muslim males to divorce and the ease with which a marriage bond is broken have caused much criticism against Islamic jurisprudence. This ques-

tioning arises not only from adherents of other main-
stream religions, but also from intellectual and liberal-
minded Muslims who, through life experience, have
learned that the the divine law is detrimental to the
prosperity and welfare of their societies.

The apologists, on the other hand, try desperately to
present some sort of justification for the laws regarding
the repudiation of one's wife. To further their arguments
they attribute a tradition to Muhammad in which the
apostle of Allah appears to be opposed to divorce:
"Among all permissible things, divorce is the act most
hated by God."[6] Proponents claim that this tradition
shows that the founder of Islam reviled the dissolution
of marriage and the repudiation of a wife. Here the
apostle of Allah warns his believers and followers that
despite the absolute right of divorce granted to the husband, the Muslim male should not indulge in this practice because it is hated by Allah.

The quoted passage, however, does not seem to be
genuine for the following reasons:

1. If "divorce is the act most hated by God," then
why does Allah, Muhammad's Supreme Creator, enjoin
it in the Koran? It has already been shown that quite a
few verses in the Muslim scripture are connected with
the dissolution of marriage and repudiation of the wife.
Some of these verses clearly put the fate of the wife in
the hands of her husband. The Koran, according to the
belief of all Muslims, is the word of Allah. If this is so,
how can it be possible to integrate these contradictory
statements? The permission for divorce in the Koran and
the words of Allah's apostle create a paradox.

2. Muhammad himself married fourteen women

during his lifetime (although some chroniclers claim a higher number than that), and he divorced some before even consummating the marriage. He was, therefore, committing "the act most hated by God." He obeys Allah by repudiating wives as enjoined in the scripture, yet he performs the most heinous act against his deity and in so doing, he opposes Allah and therefore must be punished severely according to the Islamic laws. Again, this is paradoxical.

The Koran decrees that all the evil-doers will end up in hell. Those who gossip, lie, do not fast, forget their prayers, practice usury, and even those who drink alcoholic beverages will be doomed to a painful ordeal in the hereafter. None of these misdemeanors is described as the act most hated by God. If the tradition quoted above is genuine and was not fabricated by the Muslim apologists to justify the dreadful authority of a male over his wife, then Muhammad, who divorced some of his wives, must also be condemned with the other sinners because he too has committed the act most hated by God.

3. Many of Muhammad's close associates and companions, those who either succeeded him as caliph, or acquired a high rank in the vast Muslim Empire, married and divorced their wives and remarried again and again. History has recorded many instances in which true believers repudiated their wives. It has already been pointed out that Muhammad's grandson Hassan, who succeeded his father as the fifth caliph, was known for his indulgence in divorce. In fact, it is reported that he would marry four wives concurrently (the maximum number of wives allowed) and divorce them after a few weeks so he could get married again. Sometimes he

would repudiate his four wives at once, merely by saying that they were divorced, and marry four fresh young wives the same day. One could say he was a true Muslim acting according to the book of Allah, but at the same time, he was committing the act most hated by God!

Another case, it is reported, is the wife of Thabit ibn Qays, who came to Muhammad and said that she wished to be divorced. Muhammad asked her if she was willing to return the orchid she had received from her husband instead. She replied that she was. In other words, she would have revoked her request for a divorce. Because of her willingness to abide by his decision, Muhammad said to her husband, "take the orchid and divorce her."[7] If the tradition is genuine, Muhammad here acted against his own preaching and allowed the woman to ransom herself free.

Other examples of devoted believers and high-ranking Muslims who have repudiated their wives are easy to find. From the early days of Islam to the present, millions of Muslim males have dissolved their marriage bonds. Have all these faithful acted against Allah by performing the act of divorce, or are they merely obeying Allah's scriptural law?

Because the statement attributed to Muhammad that calls divorce the "act most hated by God" directly contradicts the Koran; because Muhammad himself, Allah's own prophet, was divorced several times and, therefore, opposed the laws of his god, Allah, and according to the Koran, must suffer in hell; and because many other prestigious Muslims were divorced and granted divorces to others, we are led to believe that this "hadith" is merely a creation of the Islamic apologists.

There are other traditions as well which appear to have been fabricated by the early companions of Muhammad in order to mitigate the sharp criticisms against the ease of obtaining divorce. For example, one such tradition claims "Divorce causes the throne of Allah to shake." If these are the genuine words of Muhammad, then one wonders how he justified his own actions and those of his faithful when they exercised their lawful rights of divorce.

It is true that humanity has learned through experience that separation of a husband and wife is, in some cases, an unavoidable necessity, but it is the ease of the divorce and the husband's absolute power in dissolving the marriage ties that are the main targets of criticism.

THE CONSEQUENCES OF DIVORCE

After the marriage is dissolved and the divorce is finalized, the husband is supposed to provide for his former wife's subsistence. However, this alimony is limited to three months only, the same time as stipulated for the waiting period between marriages. As has been mentioned, if the marriage was consummated the wife is entitled to the full amount of her bride-price, and if the husband has postponed payment of the dowry up to that point, it becomes due immediately.

The husband must provide his ex-wife with lodging as well as clothing during the period of her probation or waiting (*idda*). As soon as the three months have passed, though, the maintenance ceases and if the woman has no one providing for her by then, and no financial means of

her own, she usually must turn to begging or prostitution. This occurs because women have very slim chances
of finding jobs in Islamic communities for two simple
reasons. First, all of these countries are underdeveloped
and have high unemployment rates. Second, Muslim
jurisprudence does not approve of a woman being outside of her home, let alone joining the work force,
thereby further reducing the chances of finding employment. Of course, prostitution is prohibited by the Koran,
but it is prevalent in some of the Muslim countries
because of fast divorces and the lack of alimony.

Here are some other interesting points regarding the
consequences of divorce:

1. Alimony ceases three months after a wife is repudiated, frequently leaving her with no means of support.
If the former husband dies during those three months of
waiting or probation, the ex-wife does not inherit anything from him.

2. During the three-month waiting period the
divorced woman may not travel out of town because
during that time the husband retains his right to reverse
his decision and recall her. Moreover, the text of the
Koran forbids any woman from traveling abroad,
whether the divorce is final or still reversible.

3. A divorced woman cannot get married immediately after separation. She must wait the prescribed three
months, during which time her husband has more right to
her than anyone else, including a prospective husband.

4. After the expiration of the specified three
months, or immediately after the divorce is irreversible,
the wife loses her right of inheritance from her former
husband.

5. If a husband does not divorce his wife, but leaves the home and disappears, she may not remarry for four years. If he does not return during this time, the court would then grant her a divorce. The waiting period varies among the Islamic schools, however. The Hanafi school, one of the most important Islamic sects with the largest number of followers, requires the wife to wait one hundred to one hundred twenty years before she can remarry.[8] In fact, no judicial divorce has been known in the Hanafi school as yet. The court accepts the wife's petition declaring a missing husband, but in some cases the minimum period of waiting for the abandoned wife is ninety years from the date of his birth. Only then is the court able to presume her to be widowed.

6. A widow must wait four months and ten days before she may get married again. In the case where the wife is pregnant when she becomes a widow, she must wait until after the birth of the child. The waiting period could then be longer or shorter than the specified four months, depending on how far the pregnancy had progressed by the time her husband died.

7. The waiting period for a concubine whose man passed away is half that of a free woman or legal wife, that is, two months and five days.

8. The period of waiting for a repudiated slave woman is only two months or two menstrual cycles. This, however, does not necessarily mean that Muslim jurisprudence grants some privileges to concubines and slaves by decreasing the terms of their probation. On the contrary, in the Muslim laws, the status of the bond-woman or bondmaid is inferior to that of the free woman, exactly in the same way that women are inferior to men.

9. In the case of an impotent husband, one who is unable to perform sexually, the court requires a year of humiliating probation before a decree of divorce is granted. The rules, regulations, and methods of proving a man is deficient in his capacity for marital life are very primitive and not worthy of mentioning here.

10. When the husband accuses his wife of infidelity, she must, according to the text of the Koran, swear five times that she is innocent and that her husband is a slanderer. In such cases, "the marriage is annulled and she is separated by a perpetual divorce from her husband."[9] It would be unlawful for the couple to have a sexual relationship after that.

THE ORIGIN OF ISLAMIC DIVORCE LAW

It has been demonstrated several times previously that many of the ordinances believed to have originated with Muhammad are actually derived from ancient Assyrian and Babylonian practices. The Islamic laws regarding divorce are no exception to this, and the primitive codes that are the roots of Muhammad's jurisprudence will be examined in this section so that comparisons between the two systems, "ancient" and "modern," may be made.

As has been made clear, the absolute right of divorce in Islamic law is given to the man, and with a very few exceptions, it is the husband who is empowered to repudiate his wife unilaterally. There is no passage anywhere in Muslim scripture that grants the woman the same privileges as the man in dissolving the marriage bond.

"While the husband possesses the power of divorce, absolute, immediate, unquestioned, no privilege of corresponding nature had been reserved for the wife."[10] Much of the basis for this is the Koranic view of the essential superiority of men with respect to women.

Not only is this inequality evident throughout the Koran, but it extends beyond the division between men and women to class distinctions of rich and poor, slave and free. The stratification of the Islamic community necessitates different laws for different groups.

Ancient Babylonian law also divided society into two distinctive groups—the rich or aristocrats and the destitute or plebian—and payment to the bride or her family was based on the groom's social status, his ability to pay.

If no marriage-price was determined in the wedding contract, a patrician had to give one mina (one-sixteenth of a talent, the equivalent of sixty shekels) of silver: "If there was no marriage price, he shall give her one mina of silver as the marriage settlement."[11] For the lower class,* the law requires payment of one-third mina of silver.

Thus we see the similarity between Hammurabi's law and the Koranic verse discussed earlier in this chapter that orders a husband to "Give her [the wife he is divorcing] a present, the rich according to his wealth and the poor according to his poverty."

Other instances of discrimination between classes or

---

*The word is *mushkenum*, which in the code ordinarily means a commoner, opposite the word *awīlum*, which indicates a man of higher class, a noble.

genders were manifested in both the Code of Hammurabi and the ancient Assyrian as well as Islamic law. According to al-Ghazzali, an Islamic woman is just like a slave for her man and she must obey him in all cases: "Marriage is like slavery, for the wife becomes the slave of her husband, and it is her duty absolutely to obey him in everything he requires of her."[12] She cannot leave her home without his permission. She may not go abroad or travel to other towns alone. She is not to speak with a male in the street other than her close kin. She may not mingle with the opposite sex in any party or gathering. In short, she is merely the property of her husband.

In ancient Assyria, the same laws prevailed and women were treated as the property of men: "Less pleasant is the realization that wives are the property of their husbands and are treated as such."[13] Because of this, the right for divorce lay mainly in the possession of the husband, and he had the absolute power in this connection; in ancient Assyria, as in Muslim law, the man could repudiate his wife as he pleased. "Divorce is entirely in the hands of the husband and if he wishes, he may give his cast-off wife something, or he may send her away empty handed."[14]

In accordance with Islamic jurisprudence, if a man abandoned his wife and disappeared, she must wait for him for at least four years, and in the Hanafi school, much longer than that, before she may get married again. Assyrian law, which dates back to fifteen centuries before our era, stated that: "if she [the woman whose husband is missing] has no father-in-law and no son, she shall remain true to her husband for two years. During those two years, if she has not sufficient to live on, she shall come forward and declare; she shall become the ward of the palace."[15]

Although Muhammad's law was promulgated at least twenty-two hundred years after the Assyrian one, the latter was by far more humane, for several reasons. First, according to the Assyrian law, if the deserted woman had a father-in-law or a son, they had to care for her during the waiting period. Second, the number of years she had to wait was less than that stipulated in Islamic law, and finally, if there was no one to provide for her subsistence, then the state took care of her.

The Code of Hammurabi, which is older than the Assyrian law and preceded the Koranic injunctions by some twenty-five hundred years, was even more progressive. According to this ancient Babylonian law, if a man deserted his family life, leaving his wife for good, she was allowed to marry at any time she desired. This law stipulated: "If a man has deserted his city and fled, and his wife thereafter entered the house of another; if the man has returned and wants to take back his wife, the wife of the fugitive shall not return to her husband."[16]

Both Assyrian and Islamic law treat the case of widowhood similarly to that of desertion. In Islamic jurisprudence, if a man dies and leaves nothing for his wife (or wives) as means of subsistence and she has no place to go, she will likely turn to begging or, if she is young and charming, to prostitution. As we have said, this means of support is against Islamic law, but it is predominant in society today because the women have little other choice. Few or no provisions have been made for the upkeep of widows and orphans.

In ancient Assyria, however, if a widowed woman

"has neither father-in-law or son to provide support for her, she may make oath that she has no means of support and becomes a dependent of the palace."[17] We cannot fail to notice that the Assyrian code in this particular case is much more progressive than Islamic jurisprudence. The apologists argue that in Islam, too, there are nonprofit organizations such as charitable foundations and the Muslim treasury (*Bait al-Mal*), which support helpless and destitute people. This may be so today in theory, as it was in fact during the early days of Islam when the Muslim treasury was bountiful as a result of the forays of Islamic soldiers and the booty of wars. The predatory characteristics of Islam made it possible to fill the coffers and thereby provide means of support for the needy, including those who were too old or feeble to take part in the feuding and pillaging.

After the collapse of the Islamic Empire and after the raiders were driven back from Europe, their plundering was blocked and their slave markets were gone, throwing the Muslim states into financial chaos. There was no provision for jobs for the ever-increasing number of unemployed males, much less the means to support widows or deserted women.

In every Muslim state, the thieves, beggars, and prostitutes are common and no institution or organization has been able to eradicate these social ills. If a woman loses her husband through divorce or death, the chances of her survival are very slim unless she can support herself by means other than the so-called Islamic charitable organizations.

Thus far we have shown the similarities between the Islamic laws and their ancient precursors, but there is one difference that must be pointed out. As has been made clear, in Islam, the man has the authority to repudiate his wife and dissolve his marriage bond anytime he wished. The Muslim male does not need any reason (just or unjust) for divorce. He is the master and has absolute power to throw out his wife at any whim. In Babylonia, however, the man could not repudiate his wife at his caprice, even when she was seriously ill or afflicted with an incurable disease. In case of her illness, the husband had to provide for her support as long as she lived. "If a man's wife becomes crippled (or afflicted with an incurable disease) and he decided to marry another woman, he may do so but cannot divorce his first wife who shall continue to live with him in the same house and to be cared for the rest of her life."[18] Nowhere in the Koran or throughout Islamic jurisprudence can one find anything similar to this law of ancient Babylonia wherein the husband must not only not divorce his sick wife, but he may not even move her to another domicile away from himself. He is required to keep her in the same house with his additional wife and care for her.

If the ailing wife, however, preferred to leave her husband, return to her folks, and remain with them, she is welcome to do so. The law provided the necessary ordinance in order to protect the rights of the indisposed wife: "If that woman [the sick wife] does not agree to live in her husband's house, he shall refund her dowry to her which she brought from her father's house and then she may leave."[19] Thus the afflicted wife retains the right to choose for herself where she wants to stay—with her husband or in her father's house.

In contrast, childlessness in ancient Babylonia was

grounds for divorcing a wife, but even in such exceptional cases, the woman was to be provided for. The husband was required by law to pay back the dowry and
everything the wife had brought with her from her
father's house. "If a man wishes to divorce his first wife
who did not bear him children, he shall give her money
to the full amount of her marriage-price and he shall also
repay her the dowry that she brought from her father's
house, and then divorce her."[20] As part of the Code of
Hammurabi, this was the rule whenever a wife was
repudiated.

In the rare cases of divorce in Babylonia, the woman
was provided for and her livelihood paid by her former
husband. Moreover, if she had born him children and he
wanted to divorce her, "he shall return all her dowry to
that woman, and also give her half of the field, orchard
and goods, in order that she may rear the children; after
she has brought up her children, from whatever was
given to her children, they shall give her a portion corresponding to (that of) an individual heir."[21] Recall that
under Islamic law, a former wife is provided for only
during the three-month waiting period and after this the
alimony is discontinued, whether she has children or
not.* Furthermore, she does not inherit from him at all,
whereas the ancient Babylonian woman would receive a
share of her ex-husband's estate equal to that of one of
her children.

---

*Usually, the custody of children under two years of age is
given to the divorced mother. In many cases, the father, her former
husband, claims the child after it is two years old. The former wife
has no right over her children after the divorce, and in most cases,
she is not even allowed to see them, much less keep them.

In antiquity, a friendly agreement between the wife and the husband could be drawn up in which the woman or her father would pay the total amount of the bride-price back to the bridegroom and so release her from the marriage bond. Sometimes the father of the girl, the recipient of the bride-price, repaid his son-in-law the same amount of money received, and he would get his daughter back. This is identical to *khula*, the modern Islamic divorce explained previously in which the woman ransoms her own freedom. As has been pointed out, if a husband divorces his wife before the marriage is consummated, he is only required to pay half of the amount of the marriage-price.

One might think it odd or uncommon that a new husband or wife would want a divorce so early in the marriage that the ceremony had occurred just hours prior, but as was detailed previously, many marriages in Islamic countries are arranged by parents or guardians without the direct involvement of the prospective bride and groom. In fact, the two are not allowed even to see each other before the marriage, let alone talk or date. The Shiite school allows a prospective groom to have a quick look at his future wife before the wedding, but in general, especially in orthodox communities, the man does not see his wife until she is sent to his bed-chamber to consummate the marriage after the wedding ceremony.

With this in mind, it should be easier to understand how a couple might find it very difficult to accept each other as mates. The man, for instance, may perceive his wife as unattractive, too fat or too lean, too short or too tall, slow in speech, or older than he had been told. Under these circumstances, the bridegroom, who has been misled by the matchmakers, may leave the quarters immediately and divorce his wife prior to consummation. He must, therefore, pay her half of the stipulated bride-price (*mahr*).

The new bride may also be disappointed and dismayed upon first seeing her husband, but she has no right to divorce in such cases. If she wants to dissolve the marriage bond, she must forfeit the bride-price stipulated in the contract. Even if she is willing to do so, there is no guarantee that her husband will allow it and she may be trapped in an unwanted marriage.

Similar situations in the ancient Babylonian law have different outcomes. If a man brings the bride-price to his fiancée's home, but then refuses to take her and consummate the marriage, he forfeits the total amount of the marriage price rather than just half:

> If a man, who had the betrothal gift brought to the house of his prospective father-in-law, and paid the marriage-price, has then looked upon another woman, and says to his prospective father-in-law, "I shall not marry your daughter," the father of the daughter shall keep whatever was brought to him.[22]

This demonstrates that engagement in antiquity was taken seriously by the Babylonians, and forfeiture of the entire bride-price acted as a check on unexpected repudiation.

In a Middle Assyrian law, too, the man who refused to take his wife to his home and repudiated her before the marriage was consummated was liable to pay the full amount of the marriage price to his prospective wife or her parents.

The law of the Hittites, a group of people who ruled Asia Minor in the second millennium B.C.E., is almost the same as those of Hammurabi and the Assyrians with respect to divorce before marriage is consummated. This law, which dates back to approximately 1400 B.C.E., making it nearly as old as the Middle Assyrian laws and far older than Islamic laws, states: "If a man has not yet taken the girl (whom he has betrothed) and refuses her, he forfeits the bride-price which he has brought."[23]

These comparisons between the ancient ordinances and Muhammad's laws seem to make it quite clear that despite their greater age and supposedly more barbaric origin, the statutes of Middle Assyria and Babylonia are far more progressive than those put forth in the Koran. It would appear, based on a review of these two sets of laws, that the "divine and merciful" Allah was less compassionate than the despot Hammurabi, particularly with regard to divorced, widowed, and deserted women.

Throughout this book and particularly in this chapter it has been demonstrated that the Koran is not an egalitarian or humanitarian set of laws and ordinances devised by a supernatural being for the welfare of believers. It is simply a book created by a human being who lived among various ethnic groups with diverse customs and religious ceremonies, most of which were based on heathenism. It stands to reason that Muhammad copied the ancient Babylonian laws and perpetuated them as Allah's.

Close scrutiny of the ancient Babylonian, Assyrian, and Sumerian laws shows very clearly that Muhammad's laws most likely originated from the polytheists of the past. Torrey writes, "In early Muhammadan laws relating to marriage and divorce, concubines, adultery and the family relations, there is comparatively little evidence of Jewish influence. The chief determining factor were old Arabian practices."[24] The fact that these "old Arabian practices" were superior to the Koran in many ways forms the basis for the claim that Muhammad did not bring progress to the Arabian peninsula, but instead was the impetus for a social and cultural reversal. His laws of divorce, just like his other tenets regarding polygamy, marriage contracts, concubinage, slavery, wife beating, adultery, punishment, stoning, veiling, and seclusion, are cruel, humiliating, and inhuman. It should be clear by now that Muhammad's ordinances, believed to be sent by Allah, are virtually incompatible with any concept of a compassionate god.

CONCLUSION

I have not left any calamity more detrimental to mankind than women.[1]

A woman may be married for four qualifications: on account of her money; on account of her noble pedigree; on account of her beauty; and on account of her faith; but if you do it for any other consideration, may your hands be rubbed in dirt.[2]

I charge you with your women, for they are with you as a captive.[3]

In the eyes of many orthodox Muslim jurists, woman is no more than a slave. Although slavery has been abolished throughout the world, nonetheless, a prominent Muslim writer of the twentieth century maintains that

251

woman is a slave of man and it is impossible to change this status because it would be against nature.[4] The defenders of "the dichotomous parallelism of sex and society" concur, accepting no changes in the position of woman because it would be against the will of Allah, the deeds of Muhammad, and the law of nature.[5] Such ideas are certainly the reflection of the society in which these men have been born and raised. These Islamic ideologists have one thing in common, no matter what part of the Muslim world in which they live, and that is their reactionary and dogmatic views with respect to women.

They are incapable of considering or approving the social changes in the democratic countries. To them any non-Muslim is unclean and cut off from the grace of Allah. Therefore, the sexual equality prevalent in non-Muslim societies is also unclean and is not worth paying attention to, much less imitating. To them each society is composed of two castes or classes, the master and slave, a man and a woman. They go to great length to show that biological and psychological differences prove this dichotomous phenomenon.

The upholders of the veil and the seclusion of women insist that the fate of woman is fixed before she is born, that she is born to be the slave and must be subordinate to man at every stage of life and secluded from all social activities. Her duties are limited to the domestic life in rearing children and taking care of her husband. She is denied all social activities.

Naturally, the advocates of female seclusion are men. The Koran is attributed to Allah, envisaged as a male deity. Muhammad, his Prophet, and all the caliphs after him without exception were male. Muslim jurists, judges, and writers who insist on women's inferiority to men are all male.

The shift from polytheism to monotheism with the advent of Islam may also have occasioned a misogynistic trend. As noted already, women in the pre-Islamic period enjoyed a higher status than what they were granted under Islam. The presence of goddesses in the pre-Islamic pantheon centered at the Ka`aba is certainly a sign of this higher status. By eliminating the female deities from Arabia, Muhammad not only perpetuated and universalized his own tribal god, Allah, but at the same time he downgraded the status of women in society. Therefore, it is not surprising that all the supposedly revealed laws of the Koran favor men.

It has taken the Muslim woman almost fourteen hundred years to realize how much she has been exploited by Islam. But some now voice their anger in tones that are loud and clear against male dominance and inhuman treatment. In some Muslim countries, women have rebelled against oppressive, so-called divine laws and have torn their veils or set them on fire in protest.

The women's movement toward liberation, emancipation, and equal rights is irresistible and ever increasing. The dominance of one sex over the other is inhuman and therefore intolerable. No society can be viable in which the superiority of one sex is recognized and advocated by law.

The incursions of science and technology cannot be checked by barbaric attitudes dating back to the seventh century, and the influence of mass media in the form of movies, radio, television, periodicals, and newspapers is too conspicuous to be ignored. When a female astronaut

is seen on television performing daring tasks while cir-
cling the earth; when a woman is elected prime minister
of one of the most populous nations on this planet; when
a woman delegate makes a political speech at the United
Nations and is cheerfully applauded by her male col-
leagues, including those from Muslim countries; when a
capable actress presents her talent on the stage or a
female writer introduces her book to the world; the
impact of all these accomplishments on Muslim women
is too great to be suppressed.

The trend toward urbanization will, no doubt, accel-
erate the desire for freedom. The higher level of education available to women in the large towns and cities
will bring with it the concept of and appreciation for the
equality of men and women.

The unveiling of woman and her emancipation from
the shackles of cruel Koranic law should not be seen as
impiety and ungodliness. Islam can only benefit from
the removal of these vestiges of a medieval past, which
have blocked progress in so many countries for too long.

NOTES

INTRODUCTION

1. Abu 'Abdallah Muhammad ibn Isma'il al-Bukhari (hereafter called al-Bukhari), *Al-Jami' al-Sahih*, commentary by al-Sindi (Beirut, 1978), vol. 4, p. 137. This work is considered one of the most reliable Muslim sources of *hadith*, i.e., the words and deeds of Muhammad. See also the Cairo edition (1386 A.H.); the Arabic-English translation by Muhammad Muhsan Khan (Gujranwala, Taleem-ul-Quran Trust, 1971); and the French edition (*Le recueil des traditions Mahométanes*) edited by Rudolf Krehl and T. W. Juynboll, 4 vols. (Leiden, 1862–1908).

2. See Exod. 15:20: "And Miriam, the prophetess, the

sister of Aaron, took a timbrel in her hand; and all the women went out after her with timbrel and with dances."

3. This name is given by Muhammad, but his real name was 'Abdul-Uzza, which means: the slave of the idol called Uzza. In pre-Islamic days the bedouin Arabs named their sons after the different idols worshiped by the pagans. Muhammad's grandfather and ancestors were no exception.

4. Robert Durie Osborn, *Islam under the Arabs* (Wilmington, Del., 1976), p. 91.

5. F. E. Peters, *Allah's Commonwealth: A History of Islam in the Near East* (New York, 1973), p. 65.

6. D. S. Margoliouth, *Muhammad and the Rise of Islam* (London, 1905), p. 149.

7. W. St. Clair-Tisdall, *Religion of the Crescent*, 2nd ed., chapter: "The Original Sources of the Koran" (London and New York, 1905).

8. Ibid.

9. Abu Isa' al-Tirmidhi, *Sahih al-Tirmidhi*, 2 vols. (Cairo, A.H. 1292), vol. 1, p. 167.

10. Margoliouth, *Muhammad and the Rise of Islam*, p. 19.

11. *Encyclopaedia of Religion and Ethics* (1961), edited by James Hastings, s.v. "Mecca."

12. *Encyclopaedia of Islam* (1960–), edited by H. A. R. Gibb et al., s.v. "Hajar-al-Aswad (Black-Stone)."

13. Abu Ja'far Muhammad ibn Jarir al-Tabari (hereafter called al-Tabari), *Al-Jami' al-Bayan fi Ta'wil ay al-Quran*, 30 vols. (Cairo, A.H. 1323–1329), and al-Ya'qubi, *Tarikhe*, vol. 1.

14. *Encyclopaedia of Religion and Ethics*, s.v. "Mecca."

15. Margoliouth, *Muhammad and the Rise of Islam*, p. 20.

16. Samuel S. Zwemer, *Islam: A Challenge to Faith* (New York, 1908), p. 12.

17. St. Clair-Tisdall, *Religion of the Crescent*, pp. 31–35.

18. Ibid., p. 53.

19. *Encyclopaedia Britannica*, s.v. "Arabia."

20. Ibn Ishaq, *Sirat Rasul*, vol. 1; see A. Guillaume, *The Life of Muhammad: A Translation of Is'haq's 'sirat rasūl allāh'* (London, 1955), p. 79.

21. For further information compare the following verses: Koran 2: 135; 4: 125; 6: 161.

1. Muhammad and His Many Wives

1. These were: Maymuna Bint Harith, Zaynab Bint Khuzayma, Ghuzia Bint Jabir, and Khula Bint Hakim.

2. He was born on August 20, 570 c.e. in Mecca and passed away on June 8, 632, in Medina. When he died he was sixty-two years old (sixty-three according to the Arab calendar which uses a lunar year of 354 days).

3. E. Dermenghem, *La Vie de Mahomet* (The Life of Mohammed), 2nd ed. (Paris, 1950), p. 45.

4. Ibid., p. 47.

5. P. Delacy Johnstone, *Muhammed and His Power*, p. 5.

6. Ibid., p. 78.

7. Al-Bukhari, *Al-Sahih*; see Maxime Rodinson, *Mohammed* (New York, 1974), p. 151.

8. Al-Bukhari, *Al-Sahih*, art. II, 771.

9. Rodinson, *Mohammed*, p. 151.

10. *Encyclopaedia of Islam*, s.v. "Abu-Bekr."

11. Rodinson, *Mohammed*, p. 213.

12. William Muir, *The Life of Mohammad* (Edinburgh, 1923), p. 316.

13. Johnstone, *Muhammad and His Power*, p. 116.

14. Muir, *The Life of Mohammad*, p. 319.

15. Hamd Allah Mustoufi's *Tarikhe Gozeeda* ("Selected History"), Persian edition, p. 146; al-Ya'qubi, *Tarikhe*, p. 412.

16. Muir, *The Life of Mohammad*, p. 316.

17. Johnstone, *Muhammad and His Power*, p. 116.

18. Ibn Ishaq, *Sirat Rasul*; see A. Guillaume, *The Life of Muhammad* (London, 1955).

19. D. S. Margoliouth, *Muhammad and the Rise of Islam* (London, 1905), p. 339.

20. Rodinson, *Mohammed*, p. 196; Al-Waqidi, *Kitab al-Maghazi*, ed. Marsden Jones (London, 1966), p. 178; Hamd Allah Mustoufi, *Tarikhe Gozeeda*, p. 147.

21. Muir, *The Life of Mohammed*, p. 298.

22. Abu 'Abdallah Muhammed ibn Sa'ad, *Kitab al-Tabaqat al-Kabir*, 9 vols, edited by Eduard Sachau et al. (Leiden, 1904–1940), p. 117.

23. Rodinson, *Mohammed*, pp. 196–97; al-Waqidi, *Kitab al-Maghazi*, vol. 1, p. 143.

24. Ibn Sa'ad, *Kitab al-Tabaqat al-Kabir*, p. 154.

25. Al-Tabari, *Al-Jami' al-Bayan fi Ta'wil ay al-Quran*, 30 vols. (Cairo, A.H. 1323–1329).

26. Rodinson, *Mohammed*, p. 205.

27. Fatima Mernissi, *Beyond the Veil: Male-Female Dynamics in Modern Muslim Society* (Bloomington, Ind., 1987), p. 75.

28. Johnstone, *Muhammad and His Power*, p. 107.

29. Muir, *The Life of Mohammad,* p. 292.

30. Rodinson, *Mohammed,* p. 253.

31. Muir, *The Life of Mohammad,* p. 375.

32. Ibid., p. 376.

33. Margoliouth, *Mohammed and the Rise of Islam,* p. 366.

34. Rodinson, *Mohammed,* p. 225.

35. Ibid., p. 263–64.

36. Margoliouth, *Mohammed and the Rise of Islam,* p. 386.

37. Al-Tabari, *Al-Jami' al-Bayan,* vol. 28, p. 49.

38. Ibn Sa'ad, *Kitab al-Tabaqat al-Kabir,* 145.

39. Dermenghem, *La Vie de Mahomet,* p. 285.

40. Mernissi, *Beyond the Veil,* p. 123.

41. Al-Bukhari, *Al-Sahih,* p. 459, X 68, Bab. 3.

42. Rodinson, *Mohammed,* p. 279.

43. Al-Bukhari, *Al-Sahih,* p. 459, X 68, Bab. 3; Ibn Sa'ad, *Kitab al-Tabaqat al-Kabir,* pp. 145–48.

44. Dermenghem, *La Vie de Mahomet,* p. 285.

45. Ibn Sa'ad, *Kitab al-Tabaqat al-Kabir,* p. 145.

46. Al-Tirmidhi, *Al-Sahih al-Tirmidhi,* 2 vols. (Cairo, 1292 A.H.), p. 213.

47. Margoliouth, *Mohammed and the Rise of Islam,* p. 36.

48. Ibn Sa'ad, *Kitab al-Tabaqat al-Kabir,* p. 212.

49. Mohammed Marmaduke Pickthall, *The Meaning of the Glorious Koran* (New York, 1953), p. 404.

50. Ibid.

51. Rodinson, *Mohammed,* p. 282.

52. Mernissi, *Beyond the Veil,* p. 217.

53. Ibn Sa'ad, *Kitab al-Tabaqat al-Kabir,* p. 212.

54. Rodinson, *Mohammed,* p. 283.

55. *Encyclopaedia Britannica,* s.v. "Arabia."

56. Margoliouth, *Mohammed and the Rise of Islam*, p. 52; see also Wusternfeld, *The Chronicles of Mecca*, ii, p. 7.

57. Ibn Sa'ad, *Kitab al-Tabaqat al-Kabir*, iii 63.

58. Al-Waqidi, *Kitab al-Maghazi*, p. 283.

59. Ibn Sa'ad, *Kitab al-Tabaqat al-Kabir*, II, i, 131: 5,9.

60. Al-Mas'udi, *Muruj al-Dhahab*, vol. 1–9, text and translation by A. J.-B. Pavet de Courteille (Paris, 1971).

61. Ibid.

2. PRIMITIVE MARRIAGE LAWS

1. Maulana Muhammad 'Ali, *The Religion of Islam: A Comprehensive Discussion of the Sources, Principles and Practices of Islam* (Lahore, 1983), p. 607.

2. Wiebke Walter, *Women in Islam* (Princeton, 1993).

3. *Encyclopaedia of Islam*, s.v. "Nikah."

4. Walter, *Women in Islam*.

5. C. Huart, *A History of Arabic Literature* (Beirut, 1966), p. 28.

6. R. A. Nicholson, *Life in Heathen Arabia*, pp. 81–92.

7. Will Durant, *Our Oriental Heritage*, "Egypt," vol. 1 of *The Story of Civilization* (New York, 1993).

8. Henri Frankfort, *Kingship and the Gods* (Chicago, 1965), p. 350.

9. Papyrus 141d—see Frankfort, *Kingship and the Gods*, p. 21.

10. Helen Dener, *Mothers and Amazons: The First Feminine History of Culture* (New York, 1965), p. 210.

11. Louis Delaport, *Mesopotamia: The Babylonian and Assyrian Civilization* (London, 1970), pp. 74, 143.

12. I. M. Diakonov, *The Cambridge History of Iran*, vol. 1.

13. Code of Manu, 145; see G. Bühler, trans., *The Laws of Manu* (Oxford, 1886), vol. 25 of *Sacred Books of the East*, 50 vols., edited by F. Max Müller (Oxford, 1879–1900); and W. Doniger and B. K. Smith, trans., *The Laws of Manu, with an Introduction and Notes* (Harmondsworth, UK, 1991).

14. Durant, *Our Oriental Heritage*, "India."

15. Ibid.

16. V. R. and L. Bevan Jones, *Women in Islam: A Manual with Special Reference to Conditions in India* (Westport, Conn., 1981), p. 12.

17. Ibid., p. 13.

18. W. R. Smith, *Kinship and Marriage in Early Arabia* (New York, 1903), pp. 83–86.

19. Reuben Levy, *The Social Structure of Islam* (Cambridge, 1957), p. 135.

20. Ibn Ishaq, *The Life of Muhammad* (London, 1965), translated by A. Guillaume, p. 68; also see Al-Tabari, *Tarikh*, vol. 3.

21. D. S. Margoliouth, *Mohammed and the Rise of Islam* (London, 1905), p. 29.

22. Smith, *Kinship and Marriage in Early Arabia*, p. 133.

23. Jones and Jones, *Women in Islam*, p. 18.

24. M. Muhammad 'Ali, *The Religion of Islam*, p. 610.

25. Durant, *Our Oriental Heritage*.

26. *Encyclopaedia of Islam*, s.v. "Muta"; see also Smith, *Kinship and Marriage in Early Arabia*, p. 94.

27. M. Muhammad 'Ali, *The Religion of Islam*, p. 610.

28. *Mishkat al-Masabih*, art. 223; see A. N. Matthews,

A Translation of the Mishkat al-Masabih (Calcutta, 1809), vol. 2, p. 90.

29. Al-Bukhari, *Al-Sahih*, vol. 7, "Marriage."

30. Muslim ibn al-Hajjaj, *Sahih* ("The Sound Ones"), with commentary by al-Nawawi, 5 vols. (Cairo, A.H. 1283).

31. *Encyclopaedia of Islam*, s.v. "Muta."

32. Ibn al-Hajjaj, *Sahih*.

33. Al-Tabari, *Al-Jami' al-Bayan fi Ta'wil ay al-Quran*, 30 vols. (Cairo, A.H. 1323–1329), vol. 5, p. 8.

34. *Mishkat al-Masabih*, art. 273; see Matthews, *Translation*, vol. 2, p. 90.

35. Code of Hammurabi #128. See G. R. Driver and J. C. Miles, *Laws from Mesopotamia and Asia Minor* (1952). Hammurabi (c. 1792–1750 B.C.E.) was the greatest ruler of the first dynasty of Babylon. He destroyed the power of his rivals and extended his country's boundaries as far north as Assyria's capital (Nineveh) and as far south as Ur, an ancient Sumerian city-state, which at that time was on the Persian Gulf. One of his greatest achievements was the promulgation of a law code that bears his name, which in some respects is far superior to any legal compilations attempted before him. The original copy of this law was taken away by the Elamites (the inhabitants of southwest Iran) as war booty when they defeated the army of Babylon led by Hammurabi's grandson. In 1901 the stele was found in Susa (Iran) by French archaeologists and was subsequently carried to the Louvre Museum in Paris, where it remains today.

36. Law of Eshnunna; see Driver and Miles, *Laws from Mesopotamia and Asia Minor*.

37. Jones and Jones, *Women in Islam*, p. 128.

38. M. Muhammad 'Ali, *The Religion of Islam*, p. 619.

39. Ibid., p. 620.

40. Ameer 'Ali, *Personal Law of the Muhammadans*, p. 216.

41. *Mishkat al-Masabih*, art. 270; see Matthews, *Translation*, vol. 2, p. 85.

42. Imam Ja'far as-Sadiq, *Wasi al-Shia*.

43. M. Muhammad 'Ali, *The Religion of Islam*, p. 26.

44. Jones and Jones, *Women in Islam*, p. 11.

45. M. Muhammad 'Ali, *The Religion of Islam*, p. 621.

46. G. R. Driver and J. C. Miles, *The Assyrian Laws* (Oxford, 1935).

47. Ibid.

48. Ibid.

49. The Code of Hammurabi, no. 159; see Driver and Miles, *Laws from Mesopotamia and Asia Minor*.

50. Ibid., no. 160.

51. C. J. Lyall, *Translations of Ancient Arabian Poetry, Chiefly Pre-Islamic, with an Introduction and Notes* (Westport, Conn., 1981), Introduction, xxxi.

52. Nicholson, *Life in Heathen Arabia*, pp. 87–90.

3. POLYGAMY, CONCUBINAGE, AND SLAVERY

1. Maulana Muhammad 'Ali, *The Religion of Islam: A Comprehensive Discussion of the Sources, Principles and Practices of Islam* (Lahore, 1983), p. 642.

2. Jamila Brijbhushan, *Muslim Women: In Purdah and Out of It* (New York, 1980), p. 56.

3. Darlene May, "Women in Islam: Yesterday and Today," St. Mary's College, Notre Dame, 1980.

4. P. Delacy Johnstone, *Muhammad and His Power*, p. 96.

5. Al-Tirmidhi, *Al-Sahih al-Tirmidhi*, 23 vols. (Cairo, A.H. 1292), vol. 2; al-Ghazali's *Revivication of Science* (*Ihya' 'ulum al-din*), 4 vols. (Cairo, A.H. 1280), p. 48.

6. Samuel Zwemer, *Islam: A Challenge to Faith* (New York, 1908), p. 130.

7. M. Muhammad 'Ali, *The Religion of Islam*, p. 642.

8. Reuben Levy, *The Social Structure of Islam* (Cambridge, 1957), p. 120. For further studies see: Ibn Qutayba, *Uyun Al-Akhbar*, edited by Carl Brockelman, 4 vols. (Berlin, 1900–1908); see also Cairo edition, 1925–1930, p. 436, and Ibn Buttuta, *Voyages d' Ibn Batuta*, translated by C. Defremeny and B. R. Sanguinetti, 4 vols. (Paris, 1853–1858), vol. 2, p. 227.

9. Parvin Shoukat 'Ali, *Status of Women in the Muslim World: A Study in the Feminist Movements in Turkey, Egypt, Iran, and Pakistan* (Lahore, 1975), p. 23.

10. A. F. K. Chowdhury, in *The Light*, Oct. 24, 1938.

11. Yusuf 'Ali, *An English Interpretation of the Holy Koran with Full Arabic Text* (Lahore, 1915), p. 179.

12. P. S. 'Ali, *Status of Women in the Muslim World*, p. 22.

13. Gertrude Stern, *Marriage in Early Islam* (1939), p. 62.

14. Fatima Mernissi, *Beyond the Veil: Male-Female Dynamics in Modern Muslim Society* (Bloomington, Ind., 1987), p. 112. See also Ibn Sa'ad, *Kitab al-Tabaqat al-Kabir*, 9 vols., edited by Edward Sachau (Leiden, 1904–1940), p. 337.

15. Theodor Nöldeke, *Geschichte des Qorans*, 2nd ed., Part 1 (Leipzig, 1909), p. 195.

16. Ignaz Goldziher, *Introduction to Islamic Theology and Law*, trans. by Andras and Ruth Hamori, edited by Bernard Lewis (Princeton, 1981), p. 54.

17. Ibn al-Athir, *Usd al-Ghaba* (Cairo, 1964), vol. 5, 161.

18. Al-Nasa'i, *Al-Sunan* (Shahara, A.H. 1280), 2 vols., vol. 2, pp. 263–69.

19. Ibn Sa'ad, *Kitab al-Tabaqat al-Kabir*, vol. 2, I, 131, 5, 9.

20. Goldziher, *Introduction to Islamic Theology and Law*, p. 59.

21. Ibn Abi Tahir Tayfur Ahmad, *Kitab Baghdad* (Maktabat Muthanna, 1968), p. 258.

22. Mernissi, *Beyond the Veil*, p. 112.

23. Al-Bukhari, *Al-Sahih*, p. 453, X-67, B. 109.

24. Juliet Minces, *The House of Obedience: Women in Arab Society* (London, 1982), p. 16.

25. William Muir, *The Life of Mohammad*, new ed. (Edinburgh, 1923), p. 334.

26. Ibn Majeh, *Al-Sahih*, p. 73.

27. Wiebke Walter, *Women in Islam* (Princeton, 1993).

28. A. A. Fyzee, *Outlines of Muhammadan Law*, 4th ed. (Delhi, 1974).

29. *Encyclopaedia of Islam*, vol. 1, s.v. "Concubinage."

30. Muir, *The Life of Mohammad*, p. 334.

31. *Encyclopaedia of Islam*, s.v. "Abd."

32. Muir, *The Life of Mohammad*, p. 335.

33. Hammurabi's Code, no. 170; see G. R. Driver and J. C. Miles, *Laws from Mesopotamia and Asia Minor* (1952).

34. Levy, *The Social Structure of Islam*, p. 105.

35. V. R. and L. Bevan Jones, *Women in Islam: A*

Manual with Special Reference to Conditions in India (Westport, Conn., 1981), p. 259.

36. Ameer 'Ali, *Spirit of Islam: A History of the Evolution and Ideals of Islam with a Life of the Prophet* (London, 1923), p. 262.

37. *Mishkat al-Masabih,* art. 293; see A. N. Matthews, *A Translation of the Mishkat al-Masbih* (Calcutta, 1809), vol. 2, p. 149; *Hedaya,* vol. 1, 420.

38. Hamd al-Allah Mustoufi, *Tarikhe Gozeeda* ("Selected History"), Persian edition, p. 316.

39. Alfred von Kremer, *Kulturgeschichte des Orients unter den Chalifen* (Aalen, 1966), p. 104.

40. Stanley Lane-Poole, *Studies in a Mosque* (Beirut, 1966), p. 103.

41. Mernissi, *Beyond the Veil,* p. 219.

42. *Dictionary of Islam* (1976), edited by Thomas Patrick Hughes, s.v. "Marriage."

4. ADULTERY AND PUNISHMENTS FOR SEXUAL MISCONDUCT

1. Charles Darwin, *The Descent of Man* (Princeton, 1981), p. 59.

2. *The Encyclopaedia of Religion and Ethics,* s.v. "Adultery."

3. See D. S. Margoliouth, *Muhammad and the Rise of Islam* (London, 1905), p. 457 (referencing Ibn Qutayba's *Uyun al-Akhbar,* 95).

4. *The Encyclopaedia of Religion and Ethics,* s.v. "Adultery."

5. *Hedayah (or Guide): A Commentary on the Muslim Laws*, translated by Charles Hamilton (Lahore, 1975), vol. 2, p. 9.

6. Ibid.

7. *Sharh-e-Tabsarah (Account of Notabene) of Allama Helli*, edited by Z. Zolmajdain (Tehran, 1960), vol. 3, p. 331.

8. Standish Grove Gradly, *Mussulman Laws* (1870).

9. *Sharh-e-Tabsarah*, vol. 3, p. 334.

10. Code of Hammurabi, law 131; see G. R. Drivers and J. C. Miles, *Laws from Mesopotamia and Asia Minor* (1952).

11. Ibn Ishaq, *The Life of Muhammad*, translated by A. Guillaume (London, 1955), p. 495.

12. Maxime Rodinson, *Mohammed* (New York, 1974), p. 200.

13. W. Muir, *The Life of Muhammad*, new ed. (Edinburgh, 1923), p. 299.

14. See al-Tabari, *Tafsir*; also Ibn Hisham, *Sirat Rasul Allah*, edited by Ferdinand Wüstenfeld, 2 vols. (Göttingen, 1858–1860).

15. It is interesting to note that punishment for false accusation has a long tradition in the Near East. An Assyrian law code from the fifteenth century B.C.E. (about three hundred years after Hammurabi's reign) states: "If a man discreetly, or when he is fighting with his neighbour, tells him, 'Your wife is an adulteress and I accuse her myself,' but he cannot establish a proof, he must be flogged forty strikes with the rod and work one month for the King [i.e., the state]. His allowance will be stopped and he must pay one talent of lead [i.e., about 58 lbs. minimum]." See Driver and Miles, *Laws from*

Mesopotamia and Asia Minor (1952), Middle Assyrian Law no. 18.

5. THE VEIL AND WOMAN'S SECLUSION

1. Reuben Levy, *The Social Structure of Islam* (Cambridge, 1957), p. 127.

2. V. R. and L. Bevan Jones, *Women in Islam: A Manual with Special Reference to Conditions in India* (Westport, Conn., 1981), p. 226.

3. Ibid., p. 158.

4. Maulana Jalaluddin Ansar Umri, *Awrat Islam (Muslim Women) Muashre Mein,* p. 428.

5. Patricia Jeffery, *Frogs in a Well: Indian Women in Purdah* (London, 1979), p. 3.

6. Ibid., p. 4.

7. Darlene May, "Women in Islam, Yesterday and Today," St. Mary's College, Notre Dame, 1980.

8. An often quoted hadith; see also Darlene May, "Women in Islam."

9. *Mishkat al-Masabih*, art. 264; see A. N. Matthews, *A Translation of the Mishkat al-Masahih* (Calcutta, 1809), vol. 2, p. 82; see also al-Tirmidhi, *Jami' al-Sahih,* and Abu Daud.

10. Fakhr al-Din al-Razi, *Mafatih al-Ghayb,* 6 vols. (Cairo, A.H. 1278).

11. *Hedaya* IV, 96; Standish Grove Grady, *Mussulman Laws* (1870), p. 598.

12. Jeffery, *Frogs in a Well,* p. 3.

13. W. R. Smith, *Kinship and Marriage in Early Arabia* (New York, 1903), pp. 100–104.

14. Samuel Zwemer, *Islam: A Challenge to Faith* (New York, 1908), p. 6.

15. Jones and Jones, *Women in Islam*, p. 8.

16. Ibid.

17. R. A. Nicholson, *Literary History of the Arabs* (Cambridge, 1930), p. 87.

18. Jones and Jones, *Women in Islam*, p. 11.

19. Fatima Mernissi, *Beyond the Veil: Male-Female Dynamics in Modern Muslim Society* (Bloomington, Ind., 1987).

20. Zwemer, *Islam: A Challenge to Faith*, p. 6.

21. Smith, *Kinship and Marriage*, pp. 100–104.

22. Henry Harris Jessup, *Women of the Arabs*, pp. 1–2.

23. Ibid., p. 3.

24. S. G. Wilson, *Modern Movements among Moslems* (New York, 1977).

25. Levy, *The Social Structure of Islam*, p. 124.

26. G. R. Driver and J. C. Miles, *Laws from Mesopotamia and Asia Minor* (1952); see also J. M. Powis Smith, *The Origin and History of Hebrew Law* (Chicago, 1931).

27. Driver and Miles, *Laws from Mesopotamia and Asia Minor*, Middle Assyrian Law, no. 41.

28. Al-Bukhari, *Al-Sahih*, vol. 7.

29. *The Light* (Muslim periodical), April 1, 1938.

30. Maulana Jalaluddin Ansar Umri, *Awrat Islam (Muslim Women) Muashre Mein*, p. 428.

31. Ibid., p. 194.

32. Maulana Jalaluddin Ansar Umri, *Awrat Islam (Muslim Women)*, p. 71.

6. WIFE BEATING— ALLAH'S ORDINANCE

1. Al-Bukhari, *Al-Sahih*, p. 445. X67, B. 85.

2. Maulana Muhammad 'Ali, *The Religion of Islam: A Comprehensive Discussion of the Sources, Principles and Practices of Islam* (Lahore, 1983), p. 651.

3. Ibid., pp. 652–53.

4. F. Mernissi, *Beyond the Veil: Male-Female Dynamics in Modern Muslim Society* (Bloomington, Ind., 1987), p. 78.

5. Mrs. Iqbalunnisa Hussain, *Changing India* (Bangalore, 1940), p. 67.

6. Ashraf 'Ali Thanawi, *Bihishti Zewar*, Bk. IV., p. 51; see Barbara Daly Metcalf, *Perfecting Women: Maulana Ashraf 'Ali Thanawi's Bihisti Zewar: A Partial Translation with Commentary* (Berkeley, 1990).

7. *Mishkat al-Masabih*, art. 281; see A. N. Matthews, *A Translation of the Mishkat al-Masabih* (Calcutta, 1809), vol. 2, 113.

8. M. Muhammad 'Ali, *The Religion of Islam*, p. 651.

9. Samuel Zwemer, *Islam: A Challenge to Faith* (New York, 1903), p. 127.

10. F. A. Klein, *The Religion of Islam* (London, 1971), p. 190.

11. Evelyne Accad, *The Veil of Shame: The Role of Women in the Contemporary Fiction of North Africa and the Arab World* (Sherbrooke, Que., 1978), pp. 26–28.

12. Sir Ronald K. Wilson, *Anglo-Muhammadan Law*, p. 128.

13. M. Muhammad 'Ali, *The Religion of Islam*, p. 651.

14. Ibid.
15. G. R. Driver and J. C. Miles, *Laws from Mesopotamia and Asia Minor* (1952), Middle Assyrian Law, no. 59.
16. Ibid., The Code of Hammurabi, law 142.

7. REPUDIATION OF A WIFE: MALE ABSOLUTE POWER

1. V. R. and L. Bevan Jones, *Women in Islam: A Manual with Special Reference to Conditions in India* (Westport, Conn., 1981), p. 51.
2. Fatima Mernissi, *Beyond the Veil: Male-Female Dynamics in Modern Muslim Society* (Bloomington, Ind., 1987), pp. 88–89.
3. Jones and Jones, *Women in Islam*, p. 53.
4. Abu al-Faraj 'Ali ibn al-Husayn al-Isbahani, *Kitab al-Agani*, 20 vols. (Cairo, A.H. 1285), vol. 7, p. 131.
5. Maulana Muhammad 'Ali, *The Religion of Islam: A Comprehensive Discussion of the Sources, Principles and Practices of Islam* (Lahore, 1983), p. 676.
6. Noel J. Coulson, *Women in Islam: Yesterday and Today*; M. Muhammad 'Ali, *The Religion of Islam*, p. 671; Maulana Muhammad 'Ali, *Manual of Hadith* (1978), p. 289.
7. *Mishkat al-Masabih*, art. 283; see A. N. Matthews, *A Translation of the Mishkat al-Masabih* (Calcutta, 1809); M. Muhammad 'Ali, *The Religion of Islam*, p. 675.
8. M. Muhammad 'Ali, *The Religion of Islam*, p. 676.
9. Reuben Levy, *The Social Structure of Islam* (Cambridge, 1957), pp. 120–21.

10. William Muir, *The Life of Mohammad*, new ed. (Edinburgh, 1923).

11. G. R. Driver and J. C. Miles, *Laws from Mesopotamia and Asia Minor* (1952), Code of Hammurabi, no. 139.

12. Al-Ghazzali, *Revivification of Science* (*Ihya' 'ulum al-din*).

13. A. T. Olmstead, *History of Assyria* (Chicago, 1960), chapter 42.

14. Ibid.

15. Driver and Miles, *Laws from Mesopotamia and Asia Minor*, Middle Assyrian Law, no. 45.

16. Ibid., Code of Hammurabi no. 36.

17. Olmstead, *History of Assyria*, chapter 42.

18. Driver and Miles, *Laws from Mesopotamia and Asia Minor*, Code of Hammurabi, no. 148.

19. Ibid., no. 149.

20. Ibid., no. 138.

21. Ibid., no. 137.

22. Ibid., no. 159.

23. Ibid., Hittite Law no. 30.

24. Charles Cutler Torrey, *The Jewish Foundation of Islam* (New York, 1933), p. 149.

8. CONCLUSION

1. Mishkat al-Masabih, art. 171; see A. N. Matthews, *A Translation of the Mishkat al-Masabih* (Calcutta, 1809), vol. 1, p. 454.

2. Ibid., art. 267 (vol. 2, p. 76, of Matthews' translation).

3. W. R. Smith, *Kinship and Marriage in Early Arabia* (New York, 1903), p. 94.

4. Maulana Jalaluddin Ansar Umri, *Awrat Islam (Muslim Women), Muashre Mein*, p. 71.

5. Mazhar ul-Haqkhan, *Purdah and Polygamy* (New Delhi, 1983), p. 199.

INDEX